WHEN BIRDS FALL SILENT

AILEEN & CALLAN MURDER MYSTERIES
BOOK THREE

SHANA FROST

Website: https://shanafrost.com

WHEN BIRDS FALL SILENT

First Edition.

Written By: Shanaya Wagh as Shana Frost

Copyedited by Laura Kincaid

Proofread by Charlotte Kane

Image on the cover by Daniel Manastireanu, Arek Socha and Peter H

Print Cover designed by Germancreative

For Gayatri.

Silent presence is support enough.

MORE BOOKS BY SHANA

You can find an entire (latest) catalogue on the website:
www.shanafrost.com/books
But here's what you can read next…

Aileen and Callan Murder Mysteries
When Murder Comes Home
When Eyes Don't Lie
When Birds Fall Silent
When Red Mist Rises
When Old Fires Ignite

Banerjee and Muller Mystery Series
Smokes of Death Beer

SCOTTISH GLOSSARY

Banlaoch- Female Warrior
Bairn- Child/Toddler
Bampot- Crazy
Boke- Vomit
Feartie- Coward
Eejit- Idiot
Wee- Little

This book is written in English (UK)

CHAPTER ONE

'Oh shoot!' Her body braced and muscles shuddered. Dripping with sweat, Aileen blinked at the man looming over her.

Detective Inspector Callan Cameron's electric blues, with their special hint of grey, assessed her with an intensity enough to burn through paper. They clearly didn't like what they saw. 'Fifty times in as many minutes, Mackinnon! What's wrong with ye?'

What's wrong? Her stomach growled, ready to eat itself. Her clothes stuck to her like a second skin, making her body itch, and her breath raced faster than the speed of light. That's what was wrong!

Aileen tried to turn onto her side. The mat underneath should've been comfortable, but after this torture, it was akin to a hard stone grinding into her aching arse.

Another moan slipped through her clenched lips. Her dark brown locks, now appearing pitch black thanks to all the sweat, had broken out of their militant ponytail.

Bloody detective! Now she had to deal with this haystack for the rest of their—

'Up!' The word lasered through her constant pants.

Aileen muttered a few curses between shallow gasps.

They didn't sound as muted as she'd thought.

'If ye'd channel some of yer frustration here, ye wouldn't be on yer arse all the time.'

She continued to huff, a steam engine with no signs of stopping. Aileen's legs quaked, so she pushed against the mat with shivering arms and landed on her rump. She'd be able to use her legs sometime tomorrow, she hoped. 'Can we call it a day?'

Callan folded his arms, muscles bulging like taut balloons. Had they grown overnight? Unlikely.

There wasn't a hint of perspiration on his scowling face. A soot-black mop and scruff jaw with the barest of prickly beards gave him an edgier, dangerous look – never mind those defined bones. 'Ye can't ask yer enemy for a timeout. For all ye ken, they'd finish ye off in two minutes, given yer less than average stamina.'

Aileen gritted her teeth. 'I'm not going off to war. Help me!'

Still, the infernal man didn't move. His sharp eyes scanned the barn, which was fitted with fitness tools, searching for more torture equipment.

She wouldn't give him the chance. If she wanted to get back to Dachaigh using her own legs, she had to end this.

Aileen crouched on all fours and gripped Callan's forearm, then used the last millilitre of fuel left to heft herself up.

The ground quaked, those torture-buffers – aka blue mats – providing some cushion for her legs. White light blinded her, beating onto her damp back. Was it suddenly hot in here?

Aileen's throat pleaded mercy. A woman lost in the desert was better hydrated.

This had been a bad idea.

Callan had taken it upon himself to teach Aileen self-defence. For the four sessions they'd practised together, Aileen had found herself on her arse more than her feet.

The detective never promised to be a gentle person; he represented his features: all muscle and not an ounce of fat to spare. Add this to Coach Callan and diamonds could be more yielding – he showed as much mercy as Henry VIII to an adulterous Anne Boleyn.

She didn't want to listen to his instructions. Her pumping blood and ceaseless pants obstructed her hearing, Aileen only hoped to get out of there in one piece.

Callan muttered a jab. 'If ye don't do as I tell ye, this is useless!'

Aileen peeked up at him, her petite height nowhere near his six feet plus. Damn him! Her tiny frame meant he often picked her up and dropped her on the mats, as if she were a twig. It frustrated her, to say the least. How do you hurt a boulder?

He cares enough to want to protect you.

'I don't have the time to follow your ridiculous exercise regime.' She spewed a few more curses. His fitness mindset hadn't rubbed off on her, although his affinity to curse had.

It caused him to scowl harder. 'I ken what ye're trying to do. Ye can't distract me. Move! Fifty push-ups followed by fifty squats.'

'I'd be dead on the floor!'

His lips twitched as he waved her off. 'Get moving!'

Was he trying to hold a smirk? She could manage some kickboxing, especially with him as her target.

Crossing her arms across her chest, she pursed her lips. 'Not doing it.'

Callan tipped his chin, as if contemplating her argument. 'I won't let ye solve cases with me if ye don't.'

Hell, he drove a hard bargain. No more sleuthing?

'Five squats and two push-ups.'

'Twenty and ten. I'll let ye have an extra piece of the chocolate-hazelnut tart.'

A fool would refuse it. She might learn to walk without her legs. Or a generous serving of chocolate with hazelnut might resurrect her.

An agonising eternity later, Aileen slipped on her normal shoes. They trained twice every week at a barn belonging to Old Brun, someone from Callan's past. She hadn't met the man, nor did she know anything about him.

She stared at her blotchy face in the mirror. She'd been able to calm her racing heart after a freezing bath. Callan said it would soothe her sore muscles; Aileen wondered if they'd divorce her for all the torture she'd put them through.

Most people had a palpitating heart and red face from *other* activities on a date.

Was this supposed to be a date? Or had he brought her here to appease her gran?

Siobhan had negotiated with Callan months ago: answers in exchange for a date with her grandwean.

Aileen shook her head. This was Callan's idea of taking her on a date – he'd said so. It suited him. They weren't much for sitting around discussing movies or the weather. They hashed out murder investigations. Neither of them pretended to be normal.

It still plagued her, what a man like him saw in her. His loyalty and respect for his badge would make any sane female swoon. Then came the icing on the cake: muscles paired with a grumpy, chiselled face crafted to perfection, and topped with military-cut black hair. The epitome of swoon-worthy.

And her? A recovering overworked accountant who, at twenty-eight, wanted adventure to spice up her life. She'd achieved her goal after coming to Loch Fuar a few months ago. Despite being more adventurous than when she'd arrived, Aileen couldn't fathom how Callan thought she resembled her grandmother: witty and mischievous.

Siobhan was famous in Loch Fuar for her boisterous yet loving nature. Callan sure adored her, despite the constant banter between the two of them. And Aileen suspected she terrified Callan a wee bit.

Aileen's stomach growled as she stepped out of the locker room.

A hungry, wannabe adventurous woman…

She turned to where Callan leaned against the wall, massaging his right knee.

Licking her lips, she dared. If they were dating, he'd tell her about *it*, wouldn't he? 'Is your knee hurting again?'

Callan jumped like someone had caught him nicking a cookie. He cleared his throat. 'Hungry? I'm starving.'

The hope in her chest deflated. Callan didn't trust her enough to share his ghosts. But then she hadn't told him everything either, had she?

❄

CALLAN HUMMED THE TUNE OF VIVALDI'S *FOUR SEASONS*. Autumn was his favourite part of the piece, music for battered ears, although the sweet melody of Aileen's profanities had soothed him. He grinned, jogging over to the blue door of Loch Fuar's tiny Police Scotland office.

In the north-western part of Scotland, summer rarely

blazed to burn skin, although it did thaw their frozen blood.

He schooled his expression. Nobody in Loch Fuar was privy to their dates, and Callan wanted to keep it so. This small town had too many uncontrollable, wagging tongues, which all too often gave rise to scorching forest fires.

The days he'd scheduled to spend time with Aileen, he'd fought his smile more and cursed less, worry lines fading from his forehead. He couldn't let it show, though. They'd made the wise decision to keep this secret from the meddlesome Loch Fuar citizens. It was bad enough that most of them thought he and Aileen were the perfect pair and never attempted to censor their matchmaking attempts.

The office sat silent, unlike most police stations. What else would it be like in the Town of Saints?

Officer Robert Davis patrolled the most touristy destination: the loch, their town's namesake. Or should it be the other way around?

Callan didn't care.

It was the perfect summer afternoon, which in Scotland meant sun with no rain. No wonder tourists flocked to the loch by the hundreds. You'd be daft to miss the weather. Sunny, freshly pressed lemonade days were rare in Scotland.

Callan shuffled towards the coffee machine. It trumped lemonade any day, especially after a long, energetic lunch.

The sound of the coffee squeezing into the carafe filled the air, along with its heady aroma. A barista didn't brew their coffee, but a cheap substitute wouldn't do for them.

Humming again, Callan studied the small station with its deserted waiting room where he'd crashed plenty of nights. The reception desk divided the wide room between civilians and their team in blue.

Callan scrunched his eyebrows. What was that? He walked over to the desk, scowling and thinking of 'Winter' after 'Autumn'.

A notepad lay discarded by its owner – tiny, black and embossed with: *DCI Rory Macdonald, 2005.* Callan frowned, Vivaldi fizzling into dead silence.

These were Rory's notes from the summer of 2005. Where had they come from?

A tinkle by the front door alerted him. It unlatched with a groan to reveal the owner of the diary. His white candy-floss hair was ruffled, like he'd been running a hand through it, his plaid shirt – a match for his biscuit-coloured trousers – reflecting the wrinkles on his face.

DCI Macdonald, who liked to be addressed as Rory, gave Callan the eye. Then those experienced, all-seeing eyes studied the black notepad in Callan's hand. 'Nosing about, eh?'

'Curious. The most important attribute for any detective.'

Rory chuckled, the tight lines beside his eyes crinkling, letting in some humour, before he ambled over to the coffee machine and lifted the carafe.

Why else would they have decent coffee in this place? They ran on it.

He slurped, taking his time to ponder over what to say. 'Ye've closed yer share of cases, but the ones ye can't solve?'

Callan sighed. 'They haunt ye.' As they did any detective.

Looking into his mug, Rory took another moment. 'Ye learn to move on, even if it's disappointing. Although sometimes some are so close to home, ye can't let go.'

Guzzling his coffee, Rory stalked towards Callan and

pointed at the notepad with his forefinger. 'Fifteen years on, and this case still haunts me. Every summer.'

Callan saw it now. His hair, clothes and, aye, the missing spark of humour in his eyes didn't complete the image of his boss.

The Summer of 2005 had changed everything. Not only for Rory, but also for the then teenaged Callan.

Steeling himself, Callan flipped a few more pages and read 'Blaine Macgregor'.

Someone flicked a switch. The crushing weight of a thousand memories and sorrows flooded into his system, annihilating all the good ones he'd created with Aileen.

Blaine Macgregor, the boy who ran away.

He calmed his heart, although nothing stopped the memories pouring in like a river into the ocean. 'Ye investigated his missing person case?'

'As a detective inspector, aye. Blaine, the quiet, straight-A student with a father whose sole concern was how much his son scored in his tests.' Rory ran a hand through his hair, ruffling it even more. 'I wanted to find him. And now, fifteen years on?'

Callan got it. Rory wanted to reopen the case and put an end to this annual agony.

Rory's mug clunked against the desk. 'I've had it, Callan. I don't want to go through this every summer, and it's only a matter of time before I retire. It's time to try again, give it another go before I put it in the past and forget.'

Seeing his usually laid-back boss like this disconcerted Callan so much that he blurted out, a student attempting to butter up his teacher, 'I'll look into it for ye. See if there's any additional information come to light.'

Rory's dull eyes met his. 'Ye sure?'

Callan shrugged, as if contemplating a walk in the

park. 'It's been quiet lately and I haven't got much to do.'

'I let it loose on our local grapevine for people to step forward if they've got any information. They could do so anonymously too.'

Callan filled his mug again. 'We'd get more clues that way.' He'd need fuel if he wanted to put his best foot forward. 'Let me set up a board, see how it all played out.'

❄

INCREDIBLY STUPID. HE'D BEEN A BAMPOT.

Blaine Macgregor wasn't some random missing person, but someone Callan shared a past with.

He ran a frustrated hand over his hair for the thousandth time. Fifteen years and the mystery of this missing lad still sat unsolved, leaving haunting questions in its wake. Everyone, including Rory, after two years of colossal investigation, had conceded that Blaine had indeed run away without informing a soul about his plans.

How did Blaine leave town?

Rory had scribbled the question in his notes in a barely legible chicken scrawl. As yet, it sat unanswered. Legible or not, the question etched itself into Callan's mind. No one knew how he'd got away, especially with just the clothes on his back and no money in his pockets.

Not one watchful soul from Loch Fuar had seen Blaine take the train out of town; nor had they seen him boarding a bus. There was little traffic around the train station or bus stops. A train passed through the town twice a day and the bus once every four hours. Quaint.

It was easy to track a passenger, even in the times before video surveillance. The town had always had those all-seeing eyes and wagging tongues.

Callan leaned a hip on his paper-strewn desk, hand

wrapped around his coffee cup. A few sheets crumpled under his weight, and the desk let out a groan.

Slurping the bitter sludge, he perused the board, mind clicking away facts and figures. It wasn't a murder board – at least he hoped not. He stared at the collage of the past – *his* past.

Blaine Macgregor, then aged eighteen, had been bony and short, unlike most lads his age. He'd taken his features from his Asian mother. He looked like her too, save for the light smattering of a moustache on his upper lip and those freckles.

Turning to the file he'd dug from old records, Callan read it, piecing everything together. An all-nighter stared him in the face. But he needed to lay it all out first, maybe armed with three pitchers of coffee.

❄

Rory tapped on his door, drawing Callan awake with a gasp. 'Ye spent the night here?'

He blinked the sleep from his eyes and groaned upright in his chair. Damn it! Now his bloody muscles would be stiff from slumber. He hadn't meant to doze off. He'd been so deep into this case, he'd had to sit back, unknot thoughts and think things through. Callan couldn't remember when he'd tumbled into sleep or what had become of his super-early alarm.

Rory clomped in and hefted the few files covering the visitor's chair away. They dropped to the floor with a clap. 'Ye could clean up, ye ken.'

Callan trudged towards the coffee machine, eyes swollen from sleep and his head in a haze. 'What brings ye here this early? It's barely dawn out.'

Rory crossed his legs and sat back. 'How are ye getting

on with it?'

A sip of dark petrol, and his eyes awoke. Callan studied his boss's every tell. The pallor of his skin matched the white scruff that begged for a shave. The shirt he wore pleaded for an iron. They hadn't a good night's rest between them.

And this would be the case until they resolved this mystery once and for all.

Sometimes it was better to crack on than linger. 'I wanted to walk through the investigation with ye.'

Rory nodded, but didn't lean in to contribute. Instead, he stared at the board Callan had set up. 'Hit me.'

Facing the board, Callan caressed his prickly chin and crunched the facts. He had no time to shave or brush his teeth. Not yet. 'First off, who were the last people to see him?'

'Cosimo Bocelli and Patricia Adair.'

Callan frowned, eyebrows piled high on his forehead. A consultation with the notes had him question a few facts. 'Blaine went missing after sundown. His father would've skinned him if he didn't get back before dusk.'

Rory's boots thudded as he came up to Callan. 'His parents said he never came home that night. Now to be honest? I didn't peg the Macgregors as a happy sort.'

Blaine's youthful face stared back at them from the board, smiling. The small smile didn't reach his eyes – it never had.

Callan thought back to Blaine's house. 'He lived in the neighbourhood closest to the Kirk School. He'd be the first one to get to school every morning.'

Rory hummed. 'Studious bloke but apparently terrified of his father. His mother, I remember, sniffled the entire time, burrowing into the sofa like a timid mouse.'

His boss tapped his feet on the floor. 'The father didn't

show a speck of emotion for his missing son. I'd have been in pieces if it were me. I couldn't sleep the night my wean went off to college, and I knew he'd be safe there – had his contact details too.'

Rory made an excellent point. Parents argued with their children all the time, but it didn't mean they hated them.

'He wanted Blaine to pursue a medical profession. However, Blaine wanted to play the piano. They had wild arguments about it.' At least they did when Blaine had enough courage to speak up.

'His father assumed he'd run away.' Rory tapped Blaine's photo. 'Told me he'd been planning this for weeks.'

Callan heard the lingering *but* in Rory's voice.

'But no one saw him board the bus or train. And in a tiny town like Loch Fuar, someone always sees what they shouldn't.'

Rory's frustration and helplessness were tangible. In a rare act of kinship, Callan placed a hand on his boss's shoulder. 'We'll find him, Rory. This time we will find him.'

Rory shut his eyes. 'Dead or alive?'

Callan's heart squeezed as shards of ice pricked painfully. Dead or alive, he couldn't tell, but finding his former best friend?

He'd die trying.

❄

A LIGHT BREEZE PUFFED THROUGH THE AIR, AND NO CLOUDS interrupted the warm morning.

Aileen stifled a yawn. Yesterday had been so tiring, she'd barely managed to open her eyes this morning. Her muscles ached, and she longed for a nice, long bubble bath.

She had no time to spare for such frivolities, though. The ping of her email brought her back to reality. Long bubble baths were a thing of the past when you had a fledgling business in your busy hands.

Aileen hunched over the laptop, reading and responding to emails. She'd finally opened the reservations tab on Dachaigh's website and requests were pouring in like a waterfall after a frozen winter. The inn smelled fresh and cosy – it was a respite for any traveller, thanks to the handyman, Daniel McIntyre. Aileen brought out her gran's aprons. They had stains, tangible reminders of hazy, happy memories.

A handful of guests lodged at the inn. However, she'd have to operate at full capacity for a couple of months for the books to turn black.

Aileen gazed out the window. The flowers on her windowsill danced in the breeze. Not long now before autumn descended and coloured the landscape orange.

Yesterday had been a riot with Callan by her side. They'd continued their banter all through their late lunch, gobbling spaghetti and chocolate tarts. She'd never admit it to Isla, her best friend, who always tried to wrangle the two of them together, but Callan knew how to have fun.

Should she text him and see if he wanted to meet her tonight?

Excitement bubbled in her gut. No, she was being pushy. Aileen didn't want to be one of those girlfriends.

Girlfriend... Was she Callan's—

The front door creaked, jolting Aileen out of her reverie.

A man dressed in a dark coat stepped in. His bulk blocked the sunlight streaming in from the doorway, his fuzzy white hair glowing like a halo.

Limping towards the reception desk, he asked in a

strong burr, 'Is this Dachaigh?' His voice echoed through the reception area.

Aileen smiled in greeting. 'Yes. Good morning. I'm Aileen Mackinnon, the innkeeper. How can I help you?'

He didn't bother returning the smile. A beady set of grey orbs pinned her to the spot. 'I need a room for a week at the maximum.' The burr, coupled with a scowl, could give someone the wrong impression. She hadn't angered him, had she?

Not wanting to irritate him further – if she indeed had – Aileen bobbed her head, hoping her smile didn't look like a grimace. 'Sure.' She clicked a few keys on her laptop. He scratched his beard, which mirrored his hair but clashed like a chessboard with his tanned skin. 'I think we can accommodate you for a week. I'll need some details though.'

When she asked for proof of identity – something she insisted on now thanks to previous experience – he reluctantly handed her a driving licence that bore the name, 'Matthew Edgar'.

It placed him in his mid-fifties and – Aileen blew a raspberry – showed her he didn't care for his things; his licence had frayed edges.

Aileen logged his details on her new system and used the software to allot a room. Despite his scowl, she held on to her smile. She might end up adding sore cheeks to her list of aching body parts. His haughtiness didn't bother her. She had plenty of practise dealing with grumpy people now, thanks to Callan.

Aileen plucked a brochure from the myriad ones she'd made on Loch Fuar or brought over from the tourist information centre. She kept an upbeat chirp in her voice. 'This is a map of Loch Fuar; it's handy when you're trying to get around. We don't always have internet connectivity here.'

Edgar dismissed the proffered map with a wave of his hands. He hadn't glanced at it. 'I'm fine.'

Scrapping the meagre leftovers of her even temper, Aileen fought to make conversation. 'Are you here to visit family?'

The man paused, his gruff tone falling to a threatening hush. 'Why do ye want to ken?'

She chuckled, her laugh shaky. 'Well, you'd need a map if you were a tourist. If you've been here before—'

'Tourist,' he gritted out. 'I'm a tourist here. I got my brochures at the tourist information centre.'

'Oh, wonderful.' Aileen smiled too brightly. Her palms had gone cold. 'Though you mustn't miss the—'

'I don't need yer help. My room?'

Aileen cleared her throat and considered throwing him a dirty look. But a walk-in customer for an entire week? How could she refuse?

She handed his keycard over and watched him trudge up the stairs. His left leg must hurt, for he took each of the stairs with his right.

Aileen frowned. Did she have a penchant to attract nasty guests? Had he conned her, or was he a genuine tourist?

She gulped those thoughts down and stomached the curiosity. Her brain had become conditioned to search for mysteries even in the most straightforward situations.

To keep her hands busy and mind quiet, Aileen rearranged the clutter on her desk, stacking the registers in a neat pile, and making sure she'd categorised and aligned the brochures before collecting the pens littering the table. Three needed refilling. Aileen pursed her lips. Where had she kept the refills?

In the Control Room.

Muttering to herself, she made her way to the first

floor. Her footsteps echoed in the empty stairwell, and thanks to her sore glutes, she walked stiffly.

The next time Callan came round, she'd give him a piece of her mind. What had he been thinking training her like she'd be wrestling for gold in the Olympics?

Once on the landing, the worn carpet muffled her heavy treads. The carpet ensured she didn't bother guests if they were having a lie-in, although most of them had gone off for the day.

Birdsong drenched Loch Fuar's verdant moors in a calming blanket, and the sunshine wove a golden curtain of cheer, though everyone knew such weather in Scotland could fizzle out like an unattended candle by the windowsill.

The carpet ran the length of the long corridor with guests' rooms on either side. At the end, sat the Control Room, now locked securely from light fingers. Aileen kept all the stationery, records, and CCTV footage in there.

The corridor smelled of fresh meadows, a perfect fit for the day. Aileen grinned, a genuine smile this time.

She'd designed her amazing life!

A muffled thud stopped her short. Where had it come from? Weren't her guests out?

Aileen caught the ajar door to her right. Room 7, the plaque on the door said. Mr Matthew Edgar's room.

Come on, Aileen! Stop being jumpy. He must be placing his suitcase in—

'No one should see me. I'm telling ye.' The hiss carried from Edgar's room.

Aileen strained her ears. Who was he speaking to?

He must be on the phone…

After a long pause, he responded. 'No! I'll find a way to get there. Half-past two, aye. Aye. Come alone!'

A lull settled again before Edgar hummed a 'yes' and

muttered a curse. 'I told ye. Be there.' His tone brooked no disagreement and then came silence. Aileen's heart sped like a bullet train. A floorboard creaked in place.

Had he hung up?

Aileen unfroze when a shadow fell between the ajar door and the adjacent wall. Thinking on her feet, Aileen strode towards the Control Room.

As she reached it, the door to Room 7 swung open. 'Ms Mackinnon,' a gruff voice called.

'Ah! Um…' She cleared her throat. 'Mr Edgar.'

He smiled thinly. Had he caught her? His beady eyes bored into hers, seeking answers. The man towered over her petite frame, his bulk twice as wide as hers. 'Is everything alright?' he asked, his tone patronising.

Aileen slid icy hands into her pockets. 'Of course, just, ah… getting some supplies.' She chuckled. 'Is everything alright? In your room, I mean.'

Edgar smirked. 'I'm fine. Excuse me.' He walked back in and shut the door with a definitive click.

This man was *not* a tourist. But she'd never seen him before.

Isla, gossip extraordinaire, should know.

Who had he been talking to? What plans were they making? Who exactly was Edgar?

She should follow him and—

Aileen shook herself. Everyone applauded her on her professionalism. They didn't care for this nosy cat she'd transformed into!

She put a lid on her curiosity and grabbed the metallic doorknob.

Sliding into the room, Aileen got back to work.

CHAPTER TWO

Patricia Adair lived in a tiny apartment over her electrician's shop. Like Callan, she loved to work.

The history he shared with her made his skin itch.

Two years of his life at the most foolish age, he'd spent running in circles around her. What had he been thinking?

And now, according to Rory, she'd been the last person to see Blaine before he disappeared. And he'd never known.

Before he cut the engine, a shrill droning rumbled inside Patricia's shop.

Bloody hell!

His breath stuttered and his shoulders bunched up.

He'd promised Rory. He had to do this.

Callan peered through the window to see the tall blond woman bent over a mess of wires and cables attached to an oven. She muttered to herself as she dug into the blob.

With rigid fingers, he knocked against the grimy glass, startling her into spewing a string of expletives. She spotted him on the other side of the door and blushed a deep red. 'Oh, I'm sorry.'

He pulled out his badge. Maybe formality might help smooth out the awkwardness. They had hardly spoken in the last decade and a half – since she'd gone off to marry another man.

She rolled her grey eyes. 'I know who you are, Callan. What brings you by?'

Callan bided his time, inspecting the various bits and bobs scattered around her shop while he evened out his heart rate.

A box full of testers sat on a shelf; another held pliers, and a couple of wrenches littered her work desk. She had always been a messy person, which suited him fine. Until her chaos had slipped into their relationship.

He cleared his throat to stay in the present and centre his thoughts.

Case. Focus!

'Blaine Macgregor. We're investigating his case again.'

Patricia bobbed her head and sauntered back to her work desk, blond hair swaying behind her. 'I see. I heard about it this morning at Isla's Bakery. What do you want to know about him? As I recall, you two were attached at the hip.'

To make her point, she hitched a hip on the desk.

Callan made a show of consulting his notes, despite his photographic memory. 'And apparently you and Cosimo were the last people to see him.'

The tester in her hand clattered to the wooden desk, and she shot Callan an intense stare. 'So?' The word pierced the space like a pin to a balloon.

The stench of burned rubber hung low in this tiny shop. Had the balloon deflated?

'Do ye recall where and how ye met him? When ye last saw him?'

She chuckled dryly. 'You don't want to know.'

He stifled the urge to roll his eyes. What had he seen in this woman fifteen years ago? Her ego and drama smothered those close to her. He'd been a victim before. Now he cared little for her theatrics.

'I need to ken.'

Patricia lifted her hands like a diva. 'You brought this on yourself.' Crossing her arms, she smirked as if letting him in on a scandalous secret. 'Cosimo and I were on a date. Blaine gatecrashed it. When storm clouds gathered in the sky, Cosimo, being a compassionate lad, offered to take Blaine home.'

A pin pierced Callan's heart, the pain tangible.

Stuck in bed, aged eighteen, he'd waited for Patricia to come visit him as any girlfriend might.

Drama and ego. She'd never cared.

What a blind eejit he'd been! At least he'd grown up since then.

His thoughts were written in bold on his stupid face. Patricia scoffed. 'I told you to stay out of it. Nothing about us personified pleasant, did it? The summer before we left for uni, last one to be carefree, and you weren't there to enjoy it with me.'

More than a decade had passed, but Callan's heart sizzled at her snide remark. 'The bloody accident put my arse in the damn hospital, shackled to a bed, Patricia!'

Callan hissed to keep the betrayal at bay. Blaine. This visit had nothing to do with them.

Patricia tossed her hair over her shoulder. 'At eighteen, I had so many dreams! You knew them all. I wanted to travel the world. I couldn't see the world strapped to a one-legged arsehole, could I?'

Her words were a slap to his face.

One-legged arsehole?

Yes, *that* had happened fifteen years ago.

Callan swallowed the bile rising at a dangerous pace and capped those memories before the box could open. He didn't want to get ugly with his emotions.

Back to work, Cameron!

'Where did ye drop Blaine off?'

She waved her hand like it didn't matter. She'd featured Blaine as a pawn in her dramas. 'His house, I think. We dropped him off first so we'd have our privacy.'

Callan had known she'd play him like a well-tuned guitar, so he let her jab slide. Her betrayal didn't hurt as much as his blindness to it. He didn't care what they'd done on their date. Blaine mattered to him.

'Where did ye run into Blaine?'

'Cosimo and I had a picnic by the loch. He came out of nowhere and spoiled the best date ever.'

❄

BACK IN HIS CAR, CALLAN GRIPPED THE STEERING WHEEL tight.

One-legged arsehole.

Was it how everyone thought of him? What Aileen saw him as?

Were their dates a charity for her? A favour to Isla to boost his ego?

Callan ran a trembling hand through his hair.

No wonder she always coaxed him to talk about his leg – or lack thereof. It must embarrass her to be seen with him. He'd heard those remarks before from past relationships…

His phone pinged, and Aileen's name lit up the screen.

No, he didn't want to meet her for dinner tonight. He didn't want to let her in, because her power over him? It raged a thousand times stronger than Patricia's ever had, and they'd known each other for less than a year.

Callan turned the key in the ignition. He needed a jog – desperately.

❄

CALLAN RAN FULL THROTTLE, YET THE EXERCISE DIDN'T burn off the hurt, the anger and the questions. What had Blaine been doing at the loch? The lad didn't like hikes or walking, certainly not on a treacherous road like the one leading to the loch.

He increased his pace, trying to stifle the thoughts in his mind. But the more he bottled them, the more they threatened to burst.

The soft ground propelled him to run faster, harder. He avoided the stray branches and cluster of dry leaves. The Highland scenery, with the mighty mountains in the distance, the earthiness in the air and the grey mirror-like loch, usually helped him cool off. Not today.

Why the loch? Did Blaine have plans to drown himself?

Callan's steps faltered. Righting himself, he sprinted faster still, his thoughts turning to Aileen.

What a woman! Smart, beautiful and fun in a quirky way. She made him light up like a firework. She'd called her life 'riskless' yet she personified trouble – there was never a dull moment with the feisty brunette.

His dangerous thoughts cut off when he heard another set of footsteps behind him. Heavy panting followed soon after.

Callan gritted his teeth. He hated company, even if they were joggers passing him by.

His punishment for skipping out on his pre-dawn jog.

Now he had to endure this, dressed in his long tracksuit bottoms and shirt – all in black of course. He didn't own any other colour.

Shorts would be so much better, but they were also more revealing.

'Cameron!' the voice squeaked, familiar and unwelcome to the same extent.

Callan snarled low in his throat and continued at his fast pace.

'Hey!'

The voice gained on him, footsteps pounding faster.

Damn it! The last person he needed to meet: Dr Gerald Erwin, another pal from the past.

He sprinted, calling out repeatedly, then slowed to a jog when he drew alongside Callan, all the while panting heavily. 'Heard ye reopened Blaine's case. Good lad he was.'

Callan hummed, wanting to be alone, but Gerald didn't bother with Callan's lack of enthusiasm.

He swiped at the sweat clinging to his bushy eyebrows. 'I tried to think back to the last time I saw him. To be honest, I recall that week, hell, that day, like a movie I've watched several times. Remember how we'd turned the big one and eight? Legal to drive and have a drink.' He waved his hand. 'Separately, of course. We behaved responsibly even then.'

Callan merely pressed his lips together, calming himself with the petrichor of the Highlands. It eased the throbbing stress to some degree. His legs threatened to bolt – he didn't want to talk about the bloody case. What happened to the right to a clean environment *without interruptions*?

'The first week in August fifteen years ago, the forecast said it would rain. We thought we could brave the storm. Immortal teens, right?' Gerald chuckled, lost in his own world with not a care to what Callan thought. 'Hailey Noah, Jason Mitso, Blaine, and I, we'd made plans to go camping on the other side of the loch. To goof around, watch the stars before we all took off for our dreams. I couldn't wait for medical school. Getting my life started, you know. At the last moment, Blaine bailed, said he had to go meet his piano teacher. He sounded distraught and urgent.'

The doctor's sharp eyes met Callan's as they strode through the trail. Callan didn't even pant. His muscles craved more. Hell, why couldn't he jog without being bogged down by his blasted past?

'Never saw him again. The others, Patricia and Cosimo excluded, went to the other side of the loch to camp. Pat and Cosimo were on a date.'

Callan made a mental note of all Gerald said like print on paper, then waved towards the car park. His private time with the mountains was over. 'I need to get back.'

Gerald grinned a thousand-watt smile. 'Of course! Back to keeping us safe. Hey, I have to say, it's commendable.'

Callan arched an eyebrow. Where had a compliment come from? He'd never heard one in the twenty years he'd known the man.

'Thank ye.'

Gerald waved it off. 'It's impressive how you keep yourself fit, despite having to cart a prosthetic leg around. I always give my patients your example.'

Callan stopped cold and peered into his dark hazel eyes. Was he rubbing salt on the wound, or was he for real?

No time to ponder on these useless things, Cameron!

He pointed to the car park again.

Gerald, taking the hint, nodded towards it. 'Aye! See you around.'

Callan didn't reply. He honestly didn't understand why the teenaged Callan had considered such a sod his friend.

Callan parked in a neighbourhood where the chimneys chugged smoke, and the tanginess of detergent floated with the wind while washing dried in the squarish yards.

Rory had texted Callan, telling him to go see Blaine's old piano teacher. Fifteen years ago, she'd said the boy had come to her with some routine questions. Now she'd cracked her tight lips open.

Bright red flowers fluttered with the breeze on the windowsill. Another set of pots stood on each step, leading towards a wooden door. The brass door-knocker gleamed in the bright sunlight.

Callan tapped his foot, waiting for someone to answer.

The locks turned to reveal a long passage with an oriental carpet spanning its length. The squeaky brown wood peeked out on either side.

Thud!

A walking stick smacked against the carpet. Two wrinkled hands attached to an equally weathered face joined it.

Candace Willoughby's hair had gone snow white, yet she still looked smart. Her dark green sweater and A-line black skirt were a uniform she'd worn all her life. Her cropped hair fell to her chin. Once she'd tied it in a tight bun. A string of pearls rested against her thinning neck, and another chain glittered in the summer light, this one attached to half-moon-shaped spectacles. Behind the gold-rimmed glasses were sharp cat-like grey eyes.

Her red lips thinned and dark eyebrows arched. 'Aye?'

Callan pulled out his badge. 'DI Callan Cameron.'

She pursed her lips until they all but disappeared under the wrinkles. 'This is about Blaine Macgregor.'

'If ye could answer a few of my questions?'

She lifted her chin. 'I rarely entertain questions about my students. But I heard ye've reopened the case.'

Abruptly, she turned and plodded inside.

Was this an invitation for him to enter? Callan followed.

She'd pulled the curtains aside to let the sunshine in. A grand pianoforte sat right in the centre of the room, taking most of the space. Flowers decorated the old furniture.

Candace sat on a creaky armchair, directly under the sunlight. Her skin shone like a thousand diamonds. She gestured towards the other sofa, which was so soft that it swallowed him. He fidgeted to sit straight, with little success.

Without his asking, and before he could get his notepad out, she began. 'I told the officer who came around, Blaine had come to ask me about a composition. He practised diligently, never missed a single day. Those are the students I want to teach, not numpties whose parents buy pianos because they can afford to. Not a speck of discipline or respect in that lot!'

Hand firmly wrapped around her stick, her eyes pierced his. 'I never taught ye.'

Callan shrugged. With the reputation Candace Willoughby'd had, Callan hadn't wanted to go anywhere near the instrument. She would make her students play until their fingers fell off. 'I didn't take piano lessons.'

'Ma'am,' she whipped out. For a moment he thought she'd said 'jam'.

Taken aback, Callan frowned. 'Excuse me?'

'Ye may call me ma'am. It's "no, ma'am",' she said as if schooling a child in manners.

Unsure and caught unawares, he bobbed his head. 'What did he ask ye when he came to meet ye, ma'am?'

'I'd tell ye if I had enough memory to recall what I ate

for breakfast today.' She flicked the hand that wasn't clutching her stick. 'I might forget my name, but I'd never forget music. I can't play anymore, at least not as well as I used to.'

She didn't speak for long, staring out at the gentle breeze tickling her flowers. 'A week ago, I listened to a composition from a vinyl. And I remembered him, the frail boy. *He'd have played this piece well*, I thought.'

If she remembered such details, surely he could get her to remember a night of significant importance fifteen years ago. So he asked again, 'What did he want from ye that day?'

She didn't hear him, lost in a world of her own. 'When the other inspector asked me, I thought he'd done it. Taken off to follow where his heart beckoned – to music. His damned father wouldn't let him. So I thought he'd finally set himself free, let his talents soar. Ye should check with orchestras in Vienna.' She trailed off. 'Ye need to ask the father. The man is capable of murder, he is.'

Callan froze. Murder? He'd said nothing to suggest that. Licking his lips, Callan swallowed the bile rising in his throat. 'Did Blaine ever fear for his life? Had he said anything about his father wanting to murder him?'

Her grey eyes narrowed until all Callan could see were black slits around more wrinkles. 'I'm a teacher. I noticed when one of my pupils wasn't at his best. Words bruise as much if not more than physical blows.'

Callan leaned in to ask another question when Candace's face relaxed and she looked out the window. 'The day he came to me, he sported a bruised lip. It hadn't been his father who split it. He'd had a fight with one of those burly friends of yers. He's a handyman now, as far as I recall.'

Handyman? Loch Fuar had one handyman.

An icy shiver of dread raced down Callan's spine.

Blaine had had a fight with *Daniel*?

The thought froze his questions in his throat. Candace spoke again. 'They fought about you. I remember because I asked Blaine how it mattered above his music. And he said, "Ye hold on to friends who'd walk to the ends of the earth for ye. When all is gone, it's they who remain." Smart lad. It all ended too soon.'

Murder. Had someone *murdered* Blaine?

Unlikely – they'd never found a body. And they would've, especially in the neighbourhood where Blaine had lived.

The residents in the picture-perfect middle-class community considered it their duty to know what went on in their neighbours' house.

Old Candace Willoughby had confessed her memory wasn't as it used to be. How could he take her word for it?

Daniel and he had been tight since they were wee bairns. And Daniel had never mentioned a fight with Blaine.

Callan got in his car on autopilot, doubts and questions swirling in his head. He rotated the key to fire the ignition –nothing. He tried again, yet the engine didn't purr to life.

Bloody hell!

Callan got out and glared at it. Then opened the bonnet, finding nothing amiss inside. He knew little about repairing cars, though.

When he called, the mechanic said it would take the tow truck an hour to get there. Bloody Loch Fuar had just two trucks to cover the entire town.

Muttering more profanities, Callan trudged back to the police station, not paying heed to the birdsong or the warming light.

As far as he was concerned, the day was out to get him.

❄

Aileen clenched and unclenched her hands.

Her gaze flitted around the plush sofas and the homely, rustic walnut furniture as she inhaled the scent of cinnamon bread: signs of home. But home didn't calm Aileen.

The cuckoo clock chimed the hour.

She'd messaged Callan two hours ago, and he'd read it. So why hadn't he responded?

Her brain and gut had waged war since dawn. She hadn't meant to be pushy – or worse, needy. Now she'd scared the man off when he'd barely opened up.

Aileen paused at the picture window. Was he tiring of her? They'd been spending too much time together, what with solving that case in Loch Heaven and their self-defence classes. He had to be bored with her mundane personality.

A rabbit scurried over the grass and disappeared behind the hedge. Aileen's breath faltered and her melancholy disappeared.

She was just lonely.

Callan had a lot on his plate, being one of only three members of the local police team. It must be a busy day.

Scowling at herself, Aileen made her way to the one place that always brought a smile on her face: Isla's Bakery.

The bakery bustled with people, many out on the footpath, queued up to buy something sugary. Mothers with prams, late office goers and gossiping grandmas chatted, their blether unceasing and spiced with sizzling gossip.

Before entering the premises, the buzz drifted to her ears, like the smell of bread wafting through the air, one name being uttered again and again.

'Blaine Macgregor.'

Blaine who?

The welcoming aroma of fresh scones and pastries engulfed her in a hug, and Aileen's mouth watered at the sight of a chocolate eclair. She was just about to take another heavenly whiff when a flurry of red slammed into her. Isla's squeeze was like someone wrangling the last bits of toothpaste out of the tube. But the hug's warmth reminded her of chocolate eclairs.

'Isla! Can't breathe.'

Her best friend ignored her comment. Instead tightening her hold, Isla's words muffled against Aileen's shirt. 'It's been a horrible couple of days!'

Aileen found herself dragged towards the counter, people in the queue throwing her nasty glares.

Isla gestured to a lonely spot between the counter and the back wall. 'Give me ten minutes!'

Like a well-rehearsed dance, she made quick work of packing orders and manning the till. Isla's nephew, Andrew, helped, and between them the crowd thinned to just the old folk who stayed back for gossip.

Despite her perpetually flushed face and over-the-top enthusiasm, Isla handled business like a well-choreographed juggling act.

Finally, she led Aileen to the back and into her office.

Her office suited the bakery: The walls were cream, satiny like smooth icing. Light pastel-green shelves mounted on the walls showcased miniature pastries and breads.

The crib in the corner caught Aileen's eye. She tiptoed towards the wee bairn inside and grinned.

Carly's chubby cheek bloomed pink, and her delicate eyes were clenched tight in deep slumber. A reddish tongue peeked from between dark pink lips and a tiny thumb stuck out from under the soft blanket around her.

Aileen cooed at the slumbering angel.

'Don't let appearances fool you.' Isla peered at her daughter, and her green eyes softened. 'A demon she is, staying up the entire night laughing silly. Kept me awake too.'

Aileen raised an eyebrow. 'Laughing?'

Isla sniffed. 'Hooting with laughter every time Daniel tried to pat her to sleep. The baby monitor cracked every two minutes. We had to go placate her.'

'Playing games, was she?'

Isla tickled her daughter's plump cheek. The toddler never stirred. 'Aye.'

The two women smiled at each other until Isla frowned. 'So the *bad* days.'

Aileen took a seat in front of Isla's desk, the chair's cushion as soft as Isla's butter croissants.

She too sat and, unlike herself, groaned. 'For starters, she's begun teething. So we're awake most nights. The poor girl gets red in the face from all the crying, except last night. And to wake up to the news they've reopened the case.'

Aileen's eyebrows formed a line on her forehead. 'What case?'

'The missing person case, Aileen! The one Callan's investigating. Did you move under a rock?'

So what if Callan was investigating a case? That's what detectives did, wasn't it?

Isla had more to say. 'Blaine Macgregor's been missing for fifteen years,' she whisper-yelled, as if tattling on an unspeakable matter. 'Daniel's heartbroken.'

Aileen frowned. Isla wasn't making any sense. She needed sleep. 'Why's *Daniel* heartbroken?'

Isla sat back, eyeing the crib. Was it a sensitive matter?

'I don't know the details, and he didn't want to talk much about it last night. They stuck together until they didn't.'

Aileen digested the information, then her brain put two and two together. 'You mean Daniel, Blaine and *Callan* were friends?'

Isla pouted, making her cheeks appear more flushed. 'Oh, Aileen. Haven't you heard about Blaine Macgregor before?'

She shook her head, knowing Isla would fill her in.

Isla gestured with her hands, her usual way of speaking. The grim expression she wore put Aileen on edge. 'Here's what I know. Daniel, Callan and Blaine were best friends, like attached at the hip. Although I think Daniel and Callan go further back, they met Blaine in secondary school. The word is Blaine's father hounded him. They argued, a lot. And one day, when they were all eighteen, Blaine disappeared. Just…' She wiggled her fingers to indicate smoke. 'They all assumed he'd run off.'

Aileen gawked, the dust settling. The police were investigating this case – had reopened it. There had to be some foul play involved.

'You mean he's missing, and no one knows where he went? They can't prove he's run away, can they?' Aileen's eyes were wide.

Isla groaned. 'No one knows what happened to him. He just vanished one night. There's been no hide nor hair of him since. Everyone thinks he ran off, but he hasn't contacted anyone hereabouts for the last fifteen years.'

Aileen drummed her fingers on her thighs, glancing out at the pleasant day. Blaine Macgregor could've wanted a new life and changed his identity. Maybe he just didn't want to be found.

But Blaine's whereabouts didn't concern her as much as the brick wall Callan had built between them. It had to be hard investigating your best friend's unsolved disappearance, yet Callan hadn't told her anything. Not a phone call to unburden himself or to talk things through. In fact, he still hadn't responded to her message.

Aileen shrugged it off. 'Well, let's hope they can trace him this time. Do you have some chocolate eclairs?'

Chocolate eclairs were Isla's speciality, and Aileen stuffed one in her mouth straight from the plate she'd placed on the counter. She cradled a second piece of goodness in her hand as she hurried towards the bakery door.

She wasn't stress eating – more like keeping herself happy. Chocolate always boosted her spirits.

Aileen reached the door and went to shoulder it open when it swung outwards on its own accord, as if someone had pulled it from the outside.

'Oh!' She tried righting herself, but her foot caught in the door frame and her chocolate eclair flew in the air as Aileen hurtled towards the ground, ready to face-plant – but two sturdy arms grabbed her before her pearly whites crashed into the stones.

'I'm so sorry!' The husky voice tickled her ears bringing with it the smell of spiced aftershave. Goosebumps popped on her arms, and her skin burned where he touched her.

A warm glow ignited somewhere in her neck and forged a path to her cheeks as she righted herself, tugging at her shirt and hair. She swivelled towards the man on shaky legs. 'No, it was my fault – I should have looked.'

The man, wearing a dress shirt and trousers, crouched to pick up her ruined piece of heaven. Aileen blushed a deep red.

'Looks like I spoiled your snack. Sorry about that.' A

small smile etched on his face between his reddened cheeks, then promptly fell into a frown.

Oh crap, had the chocolate stuck to her face?

Flickers of recognition bloomed in his eyes. 'Ms Aileen Mackinnon. Am I right?'

For the first time, Aileen dared to meet his browns. 'Oh! Um, Dr Erwin, isn't it?'

His face burst into a vibrant smile, brighter than the summer sun, as if he'd won the lottery. 'You remembered!'

Aileen let a chuckle slip. 'Of course! I'm sorry for tripping over you like I did.'

The man raised his hands in peace. 'Please don't apologise. If I hadn't been so focused on my phone, I would've seen you. It's hard to miss a beauty such as you.' He blushed again. 'Er… But I can't say I'm not glad I wasn't paying attention.'

Was he flirting with her? Aileen couldn't be sure. Wet behind the ears with such matters, Aileen flattened her shirt over her abdomen. Callan had preoccupied her thoughts too much for her to notice the doctor.

Still grinning, Gerald gestured for Aileen to step inside the bakery. 'I think this calls for some of those delicious eclairs and coffee, doesn't it?'

'Oh, I don't…'

He gestured to a table near the window. 'Please – five minutes.'

At a loss for what to say, and not wanting to be rude, Aileen planted her rump on the chair and perused the throng of people on the street. She relished having a man like him insistent on sharing coffee and conversation with her.

'So, Ms Mackinnon, what brings you by? I've heard you're an expert in the kitchen yourself.'

Aileen blushed and looked at her lap. Jeez, was she a

schoolgirl? She shook her head to deny his compliment. 'Oh, I wouldn't say expert. I mean, I'm not as good as Gran or as incredible a baker as Isla.'

'Don't let her fool you.' Isla sauntered over to them, a carafe in hand. 'She's brilliant, better than Siobhan too, although don't tell the old hen I said so!'

'Gran would clip your ear if she heard you!'

They all laughed.

Isla placed two chocolate eclairs down and disappeared, winking at Aileen. She'd have hell to pay later.

Aileen turned her attention back to the doctor, uneasiness swirling in her gut. 'Are you a regular at the bakery?'

Gerald moaned as he took a bite of the eclair. 'Is it me or do these get better with every bite?'

She bit into hers, enjoying the gooey chocolate goodness melting on her tongue.

Hands interlaced on the table, Gerald pinned her with twinkling eyes. 'I need my daily bread. Isla's the best. I also stop by to get some coffee. Sometimes some pastries or cakes for my older clients.'

Loch Fuar had a substantial elderly population that showed no signs of putting their feet up soon. Most were hale and hearty, behaving like twenty-year-olds. Their clan leader, her gran, always had a trick up her sleeve.

'That's very sweet of you.'

Gerald waved a hand to dismiss her compliments. 'It satisfies me to see them smile. In fact, I'm headed there now.'

Aileen slurped her coffee. 'Do you go to the Senior Citizen Care Centre?'

Gerald grinned. 'You've heard of it, then? Aye, I head there every other day in the afternoons, and I stay until after dinner. It's like a picnic. Most old folk love chatting – unlike us, stuck on our social media all the time.'

Wiping the chocolate off her face with a tissue, Aileen wished she could just have licked it. With Callan she would've. Aileen polished off her coffee and swallowed her errant thoughts. 'I'm afraid I must get going. This was great. Thank you for the coffee.'

Gerald stood and offered her his hand. 'Hopefully we can do this again sometime? Here – this is my card with my personal number on it.'

Aileen narrowly escaped Isla after taking Gerald's card, but her friend's inquisitive gaze followed her to her car.

She would demand answers, but Aileen didn't want an inquisition. Not yet. Instead, she reached for the ignition to accelerate her way back to Dachaigh when she saw him: Mr Matthew Edgar, her mysterious new guest.

What business did he have here?

Edgar's broad girth plodded out of the grocery store. He had to fold in half to fit in his compact car.

'No! I'll find a way to get there. Half-past two, aye. Aye. Come alone!'

That's what he'd said on the phone.

He sped off in his car.

Everyone deserved their privacy, didn't they? Why else would Aileen run from Isla's questions?

Her fingers tingled, her legs itched. Hell, the man limped! What if he'd made plans to meet a friend?

Yet Aileen couldn't stop the nagging in her gut.

If she trailed Edgar, her thoughts would steer away from Callan.

Without thinking, Aileen turned the keys in the ignition and eased into the lane a few cars behind Edgar's.

CHAPTER THREE

Callan gritted his teeth and watched the smooth-talking Dr Gerald leave Isla's Bakery.

The decision to keep Aileen at arm's length had paid off. Here, she sat laughing and smiling at Dr Gerald Erwin when just a couple of hours ago she'd invited Callan for dinner.

Damn it, did she think he'd fall in line like an eejit? He wouldn't repeat his past.

Callan trudged towards the police station, his mind reeling despite his earlier jog.

He should go pump some weights or thrash a punching bag. He had enough rage boiling inside of him.

Stepping into the office as he muttered away to himself, Callan was hit by the bitter fumes of coffee. It calmed him a little.

He approached the empty carafe. Thinking demanded a nice, warm cup. Callan reached for the coffee powder. He had to sort through what he knew before heading to his next destination: Cosimo Bocelli's house.

Callan sipped and let the liquid scorch his tongue. Eyes narrowed for optimal focus, he assessed the board.

Blaine Macgregor had been to Candace Willoughby's house the morning he disappeared and was last seen by Patricia and Cosimo by the loch. According to Gerald, he had skipped the pre-planned trip.

Hailey Noah, she'd been another friend. Callan had to pay her a visit, too.

Dumping the rest of the coffee down his throat, Callan thudded the mug down on the desk. Oh hell! He didn't have a bloody car, did he?

The blasted unmarked cruiser chugged slower than a bullock cart. His damn luck!

Muttering more curses, he slid into the navy-blue car and lumbered to Cosimo Bocelli's home first.

Callan drove through a homely community where the houses were compact, the chimneys continuously puffing out smoke. It was a neighbourhood where it smelled of washing and fresh bread. The kind where you could expect children to ride their bicycles without a care.

Jason Mitso had grown up here living with an aunt.

Jason and Cosimo had been inseparable fifteen years ago. According to the rumour mill, Cosimo had moved into his former spouse's house after uni. And then, after the divorce, he'd moved back in with Jason.

Callan rounded the bend and came upon a smallish house with one storey, similar to its neighbours – middle-class, made of stone – though the garden had weeds and dried twigs sticking out at odd angles, with no washing hanging on a rope. Two cars congested the short driveway.

Callan parked his at the kerb and used the meter to get a parking receipt.

Eyeing the secluded road and the light now hidden behind a dark cloud, he lumbered up the driveway.

The community lay silent even at noon. Most would be at work this time of day, perhaps enjoying their lunch break.

Callan scowled. Here he stood, facing a past he'd like to forget, hungry yet too strung up to eat.

He rapped his knuckles on the bottle-green door.

A good minute later, he'd still received no response. Callan hissed at the heat scorching his exposed neck. He'd get a bloody sunburn with nothing to show for his hard work.

Both cars were in the driveway and Callan could hear the sound of tinkering from inside. Someone had to be home.

His string of expletives screeched to a halt when the door opened and Jason Mitso grinned. 'Callan!'

Jason leaned on the doorframe, tall with sinewy muscles. His green eyes twinkled like emeralds in the sun, and his dark brownish-grey locks fell around his face in ringlets.

He ushered Callan inside. 'Ye missed Cosimo – he's gone out on a job.'

Hell!

Frowning, Callan studied the sparsely decorated living area. A sofa sat opposite the centre of attention: a large forty-two-inch TV. The glass coffee table and two armchairs on either side finished the look.

There were no showpieces, picture frames, or even another table.

Callan faced Jason, who'd bent towards the mini fridge beside the TV.

'Drink?'

Flipping out his badge, Callan flashed it at Jason. 'I'm on duty. I need to speak with Cosimo.'

His smile disappeared, and Jason straightened. The

fridge hummed, protesting at the wide door. 'Is Cosimo in any trouble?'

Callan sighed. 'This is about Blaine Macgregor's case. We're speaking with the people who last saw him.'

Jason frowned, utterly lost.

Didn't he know Cosimo had dropped Blaine home that night? Why else would Callan be on his doorstep? Despite having a couple of mutual friends, they'd never been close.

'When will Mr Bocelli be back?'

Jason bent to retrieve a bottle from the fridge. This time he shut the door, and the humming ceased. 'An hour or two, at the minimum. About Blaine – has anything new come to light?'

Callan huffed. 'I can't divulge any information to ye.'

Staring at the dark-brown bottle – at the light reflecting off it – Jason fell silent for a moment. 'Have a seat.'

Callan plopped onto the sofa, notepad in hand, and almost lost his footing. The cushion sucked him in like quicksand. Bloody hell!

Trying to get some sense of command over the lumpy thing, he shuffled ahead and leaned on his elbows.

'We thought a lot about it. I still can't remember the last time I saw him.' Jason scratched the label on the bottle. 'All I remember is being busy stocking inventory on weekends at the grocer's. It bored me to death, but ye gotta do what ye gotta do to earn, eh?'

His recounting of events didn't jibe with what Callan knew. He looked Jason in the eye. 'Ye sure ye worked weekends?'

'As sure as the sky's blue, Cal. Hated it I did, though never missed a single day.'

How could he have worked weekends while on a camping trip with Gerald Erwin? According to Gerald, it should have been a Sunday.

'So ye never went on a camping trip with Gerald Erwin in the summer of '05?'

Jason chuckled, taking a swig. 'With Gerry? Sure did, but I think we went on a weeknight.'

This would prove Gerald's theory wrong. What could the doctor be hiding? Or was Jason smudging the truth?

Callan flipped his notepad shut and ambled to the door – but paused as he gripped the cold doorknob. 'Why were ye worried Cosimo would be in trouble?'

Jason chugged his drink and wiped his mouth on his sleeve. A tremor raced through this body, easy to overlook – unless you were Callan.

'He's been acting strangely since last night. On edge, jumping at the slightest of noises and losing his temper easily. I thought he might end up hurting someone. His work must be bothering him.'

Jason didn't lie. Callan could tell such things thanks to his years of experience, although a consummate manipulator would slip past him now and then. He had to double-check everyone's accounts to ensure they corroborated.

As he made to step out, Jason leaned ahead. 'A decade and a half is a long time and my memory's not so sharp. Ye should ask Cosimo – he has the better one between the two of us.'

Yes, he'd ask Cosimo. He couldn't wait to hear what the man had to say.

❄

HAILEY NOAH WORKED AS AN APPRENTICE IN HER MOTHER Adelaide's workshop.

As Patricia's best friend, she had hung out with them all, back in the day, and many a time, she'd carry a sketchpad with her, keenly observing and recreating whatever she was drawing with just a few strokes on paper. Her reserved nature gave her a mystical aura.

She'd also never left town, smothering her big dreams.

Callan pulled into a short driveway. This one devoid of cars.

There were two stone structures, or what had been one structure divided into two. The windows on the ground floor glittered in the sunshine, the right one displaying tiny trinkets; the left intricate metalwork. It would attract any art fanatic.

The other side of the structure was subtler, with a wooden door, beige walls and a single window on the first floor looking out onto the gravel-filled driveway and small garden. Hailey lived on that side of the cottage.

She had a knack for gardening as well, judging by the neatly manicured ivy and the verdant bushes, pregnant with bright flowers, beside the driveway.

As Callan made his way to the shop, the door chimed and out stepped a lean woman. Her dress flowed around her, making it seem like she floated off the ground.

Her rich skin glittered under the weak light, and her smile matched the wide, welcoming arms.

Callan took a cautionary step back as she came to a halt in front of him. 'If it isn't yerself!'

He pulled out his badge.

'Of course I ken who ye are! Unfortunately, I have to dash.'

'Mrs Noah,' Callan started, but she hushed him.

'Terribly sorry, dear boy, I hate to be late. Toodles!' She drifted off before Callan could stop her.

Callan huffed at Hailey Noah's other mother, Fayola. He didn't have questions for her at the moment, though he had a few for Hailey.

The door tinkled shut behind him and Callan's gaze

caught the lovely chime attached to the door: coral shells and various shades of glittering azure dangled from a circular ring; tiny bells hung at the bottom of every strand. When the dancing beads caught the light pouring through the glass windows, they shimmered like water.

The store smelled of sweet roses and thyme.

Around him lay an artist's wonderland. Intricately carved wooden boxes and clocks hung on wall-mounted wire meshes beside various smaller pieces: pen stands, decorative ornaments, jewellery and boxes. All artistically done with detail in mind.

He eyed a cuckoo clock, similar to the one at Dachaigh.

Aileen…

Callan smothered his thoughts about her before they kindled, then strode to the back of the shop and knocked on the ajar wooden door. No one replied.

Inside the workshop, various tools hung from the wire meshes on the walls. The rest littered the two work desks. With no knick-knacks hanging in here, this space screamed 'practical'.

Hailey, her white-blond hair flowing to her waist, bent over a piece, busy chipping at it. She worked with great care for a while before she straightened. 'Sorry, I had to get this wee bit done.' She turned her greenish blue eyes to his – they were full of mirth. 'Oh, Callan! What a surprise.'

At his expression, her smile promptly vanished. She folded her pale arms, hugging herself. 'Ye're here about Blaine.'

'I had a few questions about the night he disappeared.'

Resting her elbow on the desk, she massaged her knitted forehead. 'I've tried and tried, but I can't recall anything from that summer. Nothing. One moment we had this silly group and the next we never saw each other again. I heard the rumours Blaine got away.'

The light glittered off her white frock. It struck Callan how different Hailey looked from the woman he'd pictured.

Her hair had lost its shine, and her eyes weren't as bright as they used to be when they'd twinkled like gemstones. And though she'd been healthy before, now he could describe her as skin and bones.

Callan sat on the other empty stool. He didn't want to loom over her and scare her, not when she appeared this frail.

'I spoke with Dr Erwin and Jason earlier. They say ye were with them on a camping trip when Blaine disappeared. He bailed.'

Hailey rubbed bone-thin fingers together. 'That year, 2005, especially the summer, is such a blur. I can't remember anything except pain and uncertainty. Mama fell sick. We were so scared we'd lose her. I hardly spent time with the group, wanting to be close to her. I can't honestly tell ye if I went camping with them.'

Callan appreciated the plain truth for once. He didn't push her. Instead, he slid his card across the table. It scraped against the rough wooden desk, over dried paint and dents. 'Call me if ye remember anything, okay?'

She sniffed. 'I wish 2005 hadn't ever happened.'

Their eyes met over her shoulder.

'I wish that too, Hailey, I really do.'

❄

WHY WAS SHE FOLLOWING THE MAN?

Aileen groaned.

He had to be a harmless tourist. That morning, Mr

Matthew Edgar had slurped his coffee, nose buried in a book on the history of the Scottish Isles.

Aileen had waited for him to make another call. He hadn't.

Now Edgar raced ahead with a two-minute lead. He wouldn't notice her following him from that distance. Hardly any cars drove down the road to offer her cover.

Where was he going? Aileen hadn't been here before, where the woods barricaded the tar road and created a shelter against the sweltering sunshine.

The traffic thinned even more, and Aileen had to lag further behind.

But she never let his compact car out of sight.

When he turned into a sheltered community where there were no cars on the road, Aileen had to park hers.

Children played in the gardens, their shrieks of laughter adding cheer to the sultry atmosphere. Warm sunshine caressed Aileen's face, making her skin glow golden.

She jogged over to the street Edgar had disappeared into. Her boots clicked against the cobbled footpath, so she stuck to the edges.

Cars lined either side of the slate-grey street. Up ahead, Edgar's black compact rumbled, still parked at the kerb.

She dashed behind the parked cars, sticking to the fences, and crouched.

The footpath squeezed between the cars and the fences, wide enough for one person. Aileen, wary that the dry twigs sticking out of the hedge might poke her, bundled herself into the limited space. Thanks to her petite build, she fit perfectly.

The roar cut off, and a bird wailed. The sounds of children's laughter drifted past like mist. An animal raced past her, rustling the hedges so a twig pricked Aileen's neck.

With nimble steps, she peered through another car's window and eyed Edgar's car. It still idled by the kerb.

Who was he waiting for?

Aileen hunched back into hiding, her breath misting the window. Yet she never let Matthew Edgar out of her sight.

The faint smell of washing tickled her nostrils; she could hear someone humming in the distance.

Bundled like a thief, she observed the proper neighbourhood where families gathered around barbeques to create lasting memories.

The hedge's leaves shone a bright green, and a few buds swayed in the breeze.

A cloud interrupted the golden light. Oh heck, would it rain?

Aileen shuffled her feet.

What could Edgar want in a non-touristy area? For some, the old brick houses were marvels to gawk at, yet most tourists would snap pictures, wouldn't they?

Aileen inched forward to another car just as the door to a house opened. She gasped and sank lower. No one could see her, but she could see everything.

A willowy woman – it had to be a woman based on the feminine strides – huddled in a coat. A coat didn't suit the weather, did it?

She'd knotted her dark hair in cornrows, and her skin glimmered under the weak sun.

Swishing her head around to ensure no one was watching her, the woman slipped into Edgar's car and shut the door at once.

The car then rumbled to life and hobbled away.

Mr Matthew Edgar could not be a tourist. Hell, he

hadn't fumbled in his journey at all. Even with a GPS, most people drove at a slower pace, afraid to miss turns.

Her legs grew numb and Aileen swivelled on her heels, eager to uncurl herself from her crouch, when she noticed the vehicle she'd been leaning against.

A well-worn SUV. Aileen scrunched her eyebrows.

Rounding the car, she read the licence plate. Yes, the car belonged to Callan.

Callan had business here?

Aileen studied the neighbourhood again. He could be questioning a suspect for the missing person case.

The man hadn't bothered to answer her message. Aileen imagined ploughing a fist into him.

Should she wait here for him to return? She had half an hour to spare until she had to get back to her chores at the inn. Her insides itched with unspoken reprimands.

Aileen leaned against his car – then jerked upright.

It rattled behind her. A muffled thud followed the sound. Bewildered, she looked around.

A boy riding his bicycle rounded the bend.

Clank! The sound came from Callan's car, as if someone had shaken it.

Another muffled sound.

Was someone inside? Had Callan trapped himself? Aileen cupped her hands on the window, fighting the glare of the sun, and peered inside.

Empty.

The lad brought his bicycle to a halt, gawking at the trembling SUV.

It rattled again, followed by another insistent thud.

The boy gaped, eyes wide and pale.

Aileen rounded the boot and tried opening it. It didn't budge.

Another muffled shout sounded. The lad screamed and ran away, his bicycle forgotten.

Faces poked out of the houses.

Her skin prickled with mortification when eyes latched onto her. Aileen pulled out her phone when a tow truck rounded the bend. Who'd called it?

It came to a stop next to Callan's, much to her relief. A burly mechanic hopped out. The car rattled again.

Aileen gestured to it. 'I think there's someone in there. I can't get them out.'

The man scrunched his eyebrows, hands in his pockets, and assessed the vehicle. 'Erm, I got a call from DI Cameron. Who're ye?'

His friend. She shook her head. 'I leaned against the car and it jolted.'

The mechanic tugged at his uniform's collar. 'It's an ancient model, miss. Hope the detective didn't lock himself in.' He chuckled alone, his humour lost on Aileen.

He pulled out some equipment. 'Ye better stay out of the way, miss.'

Aileen idled by the hedges as people gawked from inside their houses – some even stepped outside.

A blush tickled her cheeks. Aileen peered from under her lashes, trying to catch a glimpse of the person in the boot.

At last the boot opened, and they heard it. A loud scream.

Aileen raced towards the car. That didn't look like Callan! A trembling elderly woman, her eyes wide with terror, hair dishevelled, was crouched inside.

How on earth did she get in there?

'Ah hell!' The mechanic caressed the back of his head. More people rushed towards them now; someone shouted to call for an ambulance and others reached to help the woman out.

'Oh no! Ms Willoughby!' Someone jostled past Aileen, and she lost sight of the trembling woman.

Still no sign of Callan.

With slippery fingers, she called him. The call went to voicemail.

Damnation! What a stubborn eejit!

She thumbed out a text. *'SOS!'*

Her phone rang at once.

'Wallace Street,' Aileen spluttered. 'Come quick.'

CHAPTER FOUR

Aileen had resorted to stalking. Why else would she be on Wallace Street?

And now she'd landed in some kind of trouble. Callan rolled his eyes. Never a dull moment with her, indeed.

When his car turned into Wallace Street, he hit the brake. *What in the world?*

Paramedics rushed and residents poured out onto the street, the haloing light of the ambulance flaring like a beacon above the crowd.

Callan rushed towards the ambulance, heart in his throat. The sweet smell of home never registered; nor did the gawking faces.

Had Aileen hurt herself?

He saw the gurney, and his steps faltered. Not *Aileen,* but a frail old woman. Her waspishness had vanished in the past couple of hours since Callan had met her.

He came to a halt beside the gurney. 'Ms Willoughby.'

The gashes around her throat burned bright red

against her pale wrinkled face; her cultured hair tousled like someone had yanked on it.

Callan grimaced at the state of her skirt and shirt. Who had brutally torn her clothes?

An oxygen mask covered most of her face. Her eyes above the mask were wide. She shivered.

What animal would do this to an old woman?

Her eyes widened into saucers, her eyebrows piling high on her forehead. Pointing a shivering finger at him, she thrashed out her legs and wriggled. 'Him! It's him! He attacked me!'

What the hell?

Callan shook his head. 'Ma'am, please calm down. We *spoke* earlier, remember?'

Her whimpers drowned out his words. She writhed as if she'd seen the hidden monster.

A firm hand settled onto Callan's shoulders and tugged him back. 'Let the ambulance go.' Rory's voice held a non-negotiable command.

The door slammed, and a siren pierced the steady murmurs of the crowd. The ambulance raced away, leaving questions in its wake.

Confused and now utterly baffled by his boss's behaviour, Callan blinked. 'What's going on?'

Rory came into his line of vision. 'Why don't ye tell me?'

He swivelled, walking off, leaving Callan to follow. They strode towards Callan's car, the boot open wide.

Where had the tow truck he'd called earlier got to? Shouldn't the mechanic have—

Rory snapped when they slid safely out of view behind his car. 'What do ye think ye're doing?'

Callan frowned. 'Rory, I'm—'

'I want this case solved just as bad as you, but I don't take to roughing up the people I interview.'

Callan's gaze latched onto his boss's raging eyes, and he saw a flicker of uncertainty in them. He studied the empty boot and spotted a shiny piece of silver on the prickly carpet.

He didn't need to bend low to know what had caught his eye.

An icy bolt of unease ripped through his taut body. A delicate silver chain – on which dangled a pendant of a soaring bird, also silver. He *knew* that chain.

A fire ignited in Callan's belly and boomed through him, slicing the cold. 'Ye think I abducted Ms Willoughby? Hurt her?'

'She says ye did.'

Rory's face gave nothing away. With gloved hands, he plucked the prone chain out of the boot and dangled it from one finger.

The silver caught the light, glimmering as the bird-shaped pendant twisted.

He read the engraving before Rory pointed it out and his legs lost their strength. The air left Callan's lungs, and the bitter aftertaste of poison oozed on his tongue.

Deflated, defeated…

No, this couldn't be happening. This nightmare couldn't resurface again.

Callan placed a hand on the car to steady himself. He wouldn't crash to the ground with so many witnesses.

The shimmering light picked up a single word scrawled on the soaring bird's belly in neat handwriting: 'Callan'.

Looking straight into Callan's eyes, Rory hissed, 'We found this wrapped around a gagged and tied Ms Willoughby. Explain, Detective!'

❄

AILEEN HAD BEEN AT THE SCENE, LEANING AGAINST A STONE wall. Callan didn't have the energy to speak with her. Their eyes locked for a moment – hers held a myriad of questions.

He walked away to the other side of the street, deflecting her questions and concern. He didn't want to make this more painful.

If Rory wanted to, he could easily suspend him, or worse…

Callan cleared his throat and brought himself back to reality. He'd done nothing wrong, and he'd prove it.

That chain… Callan's gaze drifted towards his car. Where had it come from?

He knew where he'd buried it fifteen years ago.

Jeez, he'd all but forgotten about the bloody thing!

Callan slid into his borrowed car and shut his eyes. He had to face the music. Hadn't he decided the day was out to get him?

❄

THE SOUND OF THE COFFEE MACHINE SPITTING OUT ITS usual sludge droned through the icy room. The smell made Callan crave a hit himself.

Not yet.

Rory's heavy treads sounded behind Callan. He hunkered in what seemed like the principal's office, hoping this wouldn't end his career.

Unlike his tiny space, Rory's office had two windows. The wooden desk gleamed, visible under the stacks of paper. His pen stand had a few pens and pencils Callan could bet worked.

The coffee mug thudded on the coaster. The chair squeaked when Rory sat and leaned his elbows on the table.

Callan sought refuge in the aroma of the coffee.

The clock on the desk ticked away the seconds. Callan attempted to count them, to take his mind off his racing heart.

A cold sliver of sweat trickled between his shoulder blades.

Another full minute passed. Rory continued to stare Callan right in the eyes.

Hands on his trousers, Callan fingered a loose thread.

'Explain.' The word zapped like the crack of a whip.

Callan swallowed the vomit churning inside him and recounted his movements of the day. 'I left Ms Willoughby's at around half-past twelve and hiked it back here. A couple of minutes later, I drove the unmarked cruiser to Jason and Cosimo's house, but Cosimo wasn't in. So I spoke with Jason. From there, I went to Adelaide Noah's shop. I left after speaking with Hailey Noah when Aileen called.'

Rory steepled his fingers, his gaze still unyielding. Where was the usual joyful twinkle?

'I'll get Robert to ask around if anyone saw ye leaving Ms Willoughby's and I'll speak with Ms Noah and Mitso myself.'

Relief, like a pot of warm honey, washed over him. Thank goodness.

'But.' Rory raised his forefinger. 'Ye're off this case.'

Ice, a bucketful of ice. This couldn't happen.

'I—'

'No, Callan, ye're too close to this case. I cannae let ye investigate it. I shouldn't have asked ye to do this in the first place. Blaine Macgregor was yer best friend.'

Callan clenched his jaw tight. He *could* do this. He prided himself on his ability to be objective. 'Look, Rory, I dinnae ken what happened there today. I didn't do it! And for this case, I told ye, I won't stop—'

'That's the problem, Callan! Ye won't stop or ken the limits. I ken this case is fifteen years old, and I have little hope to solve it. I don't want one of my best detectives to get so involved in this case that he puts his career on the line.'

'Rory.'

'Detective! I won't. End of discussion!'

Rory's voice boomed through the tiny police office, and a muscle in his jaw twitched.

In the three decades Callan had known him, he'd never seen Rory this angry.

He swallowed his arguments and rose. 'I'm sorry.' With a hung head, he walked away.

Yes, a sweaty kickboxing session sounded good about now.

❄

Callan found himself back in Old Brun's barn, where he'd last had a good time. A lifetime could have passed since then.

Those memories from fifteen years ago? They were still a raw wound, smarting every time he pictured Blaine's youthful face.

The punching bag swung. Callan jabbed it, his fists encased in red boxing gloves.

He wore shorts this time, knowing nobody would disturb him here. No phone calls, unwelcome old pals or cases which twisted his gut in a knot.

He'd punched his knuckles raw, a tangible pain for his memories.

The summer day had descended into a windy night. It howled outside, and the sky wept thick droplets of rain, which crashed to the ground.

Mother Nature echoed his sentiments.

When a sharp zing of pain shot through his arm, Callan let his clenched fist loosen. His panting joined the rhythm of the downpour. The barn smelled of rubber mats.

His black vest showed off his sweaty muscles; his dark hair, matted with more sweat, glistening under the white light.

Candace said she'd seen *him*. She said *he'd* abducted her, hurt her, and stuffed her in his car.

Callan would never harm a woman – a lesson he'd learned early when his mother had skinned his hide for cat-calling a classmate. He never crossed that line, despite threatening Aileen whenever she got on his nerves.

Callan ran a hand through his hair, displacing the droplets which ran into his eyes, yet the raw sting in his heart fuelled him.

Jab-cross-jab-cross-knee.

He kept at it.

It numbed his mind and brought the clarity he needed.

The chain they'd found with Candace he'd buried fifteen years ago. Everyone in their group had owned the same chain, paired with a red T-shirt with a bird logo on it. They'd called themselves the 'White Birds' – birds waiting to soar and colour their wings.

Who'd found his chain? How did it shine after all these years?

Callan paused mid-punch. This meant whoever had

kidnapped Candace knew about the chains or had a chain themselves.

The weight of that thought crushed all his fight. It meant his former friends were now suspects in a kidnapping and assault case. Yet the target hadn't been the frail old piano teacher. Someone had targeted him. *Framed him.*

The realisation was akin to the force of a hundred bullets: sharp and painful.

It steeled Callan's resolve.

Rory might have pushed him off the case, but Callan knew his capabilities. He could be objective and find his best friend.

He'd show these eejits what happened when they messed with Detective Inspector Callan Cameron.

❄

WORRY ROILED IN AILEEN'S GUT.

The way Rory had snapped at Callan and then dragged him off to the police station didn't sit right with her. He should know Callan wouldn't hurt an old woman. Despite his gruff exterior, Callan never mistreated an innocent.

He was the sort who worked his arse off, would put his life on the line to save someone he didn't know, and held the utmost respect for his badge.

She'd seen him work tirelessly for justice.

Aileen reread the messages she'd sent him since yesterday. Goodness, had their self-defence class only been yesterday?

It stormed outside now, the night vicious.

When Callan had hung his head, refusing to meet her gaze for more than a moment on Wallace Street, she'd known he blamed himself.

Had Rory suspended him?

Aileen had driven by the police station, where Robert had informed her Callan had taken off.

Callan never cut his shift early.

When her five calls went unanswered, she was left with no hope that he'd respond tonight.

Was he angry at her or the situation? Or both?

Aileen peered outside the window to meet with blackness and her frowning face.

Callan didn't want her around anymore. She'd bored him with her nagging.

Aileen rubbed her tired eyes. She should call it a day.

Patting her right trouser pocket, she ensured her keys were where she'd put them. Then, meticulously, she locked up.

Aileen checked the two doors and the windows before heading towards the library. There was no one cosied in with a book, so she headed for the small table between the two high-backed chairs she'd recently added.

An antique lamp sat on the wooden coffee table. Its warm glow gave the library a dreamy look: a place that could whisk one away on adventures.

She bent over the lamp to switch it off when she noticed it – a mobile phone.

Which of her guests might have left it behind?

Aileen picked it off the table when the screen illuminated. The smartphone belonged to an older series and fit in her palm.

Of course there would be no name on the device. It needed to go in the lost and—

'Willing to buy in cash. I think you should take it and leave LF immediately.'

Aileen stopped short when her eyes habitually read the text. Buy in cash? LF as in Loch Fuar? Leave?

Swallowing, she glanced over her shoulder. All sat still.

Aileen scrolled through the notifications with clammy fingers until she came to the next message.

'Whoever it was is active again. You best get out.'

Who'd become active? Apparently, the sender didn't know.

The sender hadn't signed the messages, nor had the phone's owner saved this number. The code belonged to the UK, though.

Another message popped up in the notifications from the same sender.

'The old hag got it. Locked in the boot apparently.'

Aileen gasped. She knew of one person found in a boot of a car. *She* had found her.

Hands ice-cold and heart palpitating like a racing engine, Aileen's gaze flitted around the room.

She pressed the home button, but the phone demanded a password.

Hell!

Aileen licked her lips and stared at the messages again.

'Ms Mackinnon.'

She jolted, swivelling to face the voice. 'Mr... Mr Edgar. Um, is... is this your phone?' she spluttered.

Those beady eyes held hers, zeroing in on the phone in her hand. 'Aye, it's mine. Hasn't anyone told ye it's unethical to go through yer guests' belongings?'

She wiped her hands on her trousers. 'I wasn't... I was locking up when I saw the phone. I'd have logged it into lost and found.'

Edgar's boots snapped over the floor as he took a step towards her and snatched the phone from her hands like a teacher confiscating an errant lipstick. 'I'm not in the habit of losing my phone, Ms Mackinnon. Nor do I need a secretary to go through my messages.'

'I… I…'

Edgar turned on his heels and clambered up the stairs.

Aileen huffed; her skills were rusty. Her sleuthing skills needed to be oiled again.

Something didn't sit right with Edgar, and she'd find out what. No matter how long it took.

❄

THE NEXT MORNING, AILEEN SAT BEFORE HER LAPTOP, chewing on her bottom lip before giving in and tapping the name in.

'Matthew Edgar.'

She couldn't resist…

It took her an hour of pointless browsing to table the research. There were too many Matthew Edgars to find the one currently staying under her roof. There were no images to find on any social networks or on the web. Aileen snapped the laptop shut to make her way to a more resourceful hub of information – Isla's Bakery.

The sun played peek-a-boo with the clouds; the roads damp after last night's storm, dew drops glittering on the grass like stars.

A light breeze tickled Aileen's hair as the warmth of bread loaves hit her.

The bakery brimmed with people. And her friend danced in her element, packaging orders, manning the till and exchanging piping hot gossip all at once.

Now used to the energetic redhead, Aileen braced herself as Isla rounded the counter and slammed into her.

Isla squashed her as tight as always. Aileen's lungs had become accustomed to this daily squeezing.

Aileen loved Isla's enthusiasm – the woman hugged you like she hadn't seen you in years.

Without waiting for a greeting, her friend jumped right in. 'Did you hear about poor Candace Willoughby? And did you know the sod bumped her in Callan's car? Mr Ferguson said…'

Aileen patted her friend's back. 'Breathe, Isla. Breathe.'

Isla shook her wild hair, a grin erupting between her flushed cheeks. 'Of course, you know. You were there! And I want to know all about it.' She dragged Aileen behind the counter and into her tiny office.

The crib in the corner sat empty, much to Aileen's disappointment. She focused on the fiend sitting behind the desk instead. 'What about all those customers?' Aileen jabbed a thumb at the rush outside.

Isla waved her hand. 'They'll wait until Andrew gets to them. Hell, I need to increase staff, and Daniel says he can work on expanding the shop. Did you know, the space next to this one is coming up for sale? Should I make an offer?'

Aileen blinked. 'It's more like a necessity at this point unless you want people to queue the entire night to get their morning bread.'

Isla huffed and swatted a stray strand from her eyes. 'Enough about business – you've got more sizzling hot tales to tell. Coffee date with Dr Gerald Erwin. Then there's DI Callan Cameron. Look at you, Ms Mackinnon – two men vying for your attention.'

Aileen's eye roll sent Isla chuckling.

'Do tell.'

Of course Isla would grill her about this. Aileen had known that, yet she'd forgotten about Gerald after her crazy afternoon. Besides, she didn't need two men; she needed one. And like a glutton for punishment, she needed the one who was ignoring her.

'Don't start. The doctor did the polite thing after I bumped into him. I told him he didn't have to.'

'He's interested in you, Aileen!' Isla knocked her knuckles on the desk. 'Open your eyes, woman!'

Aileen mimed rounding her eyes to resemble saucers. 'Wide awake, Mrs McIntyre.'

They both giggled. Aileen felt lucky to have a friend she could be silly with.

At the mention of friends, it dawned on her. 'Has Callan spoken to Daniel?'

The smile vanished from Isla's face. 'Men aren't the sort to share their feelings, and Callan tops the list. It would take a crowbar to pry his mouth open.'

No one had ever spoken truer words.

Aileen sighed. 'I think what happened with Ms Willoughby…' She didn't know what to say. Not even Isla knew Aileen and Callan were secretly sort of dating. Though dating or not, Aileen cared about him a great deal.

'I know what you mean. He goes to interview her about his missing best friend and in a matter of hours, she's found in the boot of his car. Add it to the pressure of the case. It must be hard.'

Aileen's heart picked its pace. 'Did Rory suspend him?'

Isla hung her head, yet her eyes held a mischievous glint. 'Why don't you call him?'

Almost everyone in Loch Fuar wanted them together, and no one probed tactfully.

The constant intrusion into her privacy didn't come as a surprise – not anymore. She'd come to expect it now. Aileen blew a raspberry. 'I tried – he isn't answering my calls or messages.'

Isla pouted. 'Lovers' quarrel?'

'No. No, we didn't quarrel.' Aileen waved her hands. 'One minute he's friendly, and the next he doesn't bother responding to my messages. I don't understand him.'

'It's difficult to understand a man who's scared.'

'What?'

'Never mind. Callan's behaviour isn't the only thing bothering you. Why are you here so early in the morning? I can see it in your eyes.'

Aileen pursed her lips, studying Isla. 'I think I'm being fooled again.'

Leaning in, she told her friend about Mr Matthew Edgar and the messages.

Despite her rambling nature, Isla listened with patience and care. Eyes narrowed, she hummed as she hung on Aileen's every word.

Then she pulled out a notepad and scribbled on it, penning the messages in reverse order.

And hadn't she been smart to do so?

Aileen chuckled. 'You're smart. I never figured it out until now. The first message had to be at the bottom of the screen.'

Isla nodded. 'The latest notifications appear at the top and push the earlier messages to the bottom.'

Chewing on her pencil, Isla ticked off the last message first. 'The bit about the old hag had to be Ms Willoughby. It's not every day an old lady's found in the boot of a car, let alone a detective's. I don't think Callan did it. He isn't a bully. Rough? *Is* he rough?' Isla cocked a mocking eyebrow.

Aileen rolled her eyes. 'Focus, Isla.'

Isla got back to the notepad. Aileen read her handwriting, clear against the white paper, with ease, contrary to Callan's chicken scrawl.

'And what did the remaining messages say? About whoever it was being active again.'

Tapping her chin, Aileen met Isla's gaze. 'Notice how the message says "who" instead of "what"?'

'Noticed. The same phone number sent these messages, right?'

Aileen harrumphed. 'The same alright, although I don't recall the entire number. I wrote what the messages said.'

The constant chatter in the bakery died out as the queue dwindled, thanks to the late morning hour. It gave them more headspace to think.

'Ye know what this means, don't ye? If it's the same sender, these messages have to follow some link.' Isla tapped the last sentence she'd scrawled. '"*Leave LF immediately.*" Seeing as the phone belonged to Mr Edgar, LF has to be Loch Fuar.'

Isla's accent thickened the more excited she got.

Aileen sat back in her chair. 'Yes, it is. What could be so dangerous here? This person asks him twice "to get out" and "leave immediately".'

Isla drummed her fingers on the desk. 'Ye saw him pick up this woman at Wallace Street. Let's go back and find out which house she stepped out from. It might be hers.'

It made sense. 'Good thinking. I came here hoping you could find some intel on Matthew Edgar.'

'I'll see what I can do, although I haven't heard of him before. Can ye wait half an hour? The part-time employee's coming in to help and I'll get things sorted out here by then.'

'Would I get a chocolate eclair?'

'Yup.'

CHAPTER FIVE

Isla rubbed her hands. 'Ready to go sleuthing?'

Aileen grinned. 'Oh, as I'll ever be.'

Like the previous day, Aileen parked her car in the adjacent street to be as inconspicuous as possible.

As one, they rounded the bend, Isla whispering, 'In case we get caught I have the perfect excuse.' She pulled out a packet of shortbread with her packaging on it. 'Don't most people get lost making deliveries?'

They discreetly clapped their hands. Brilliant excuse!

'We're taking the air. It's not illegal, is it?'

A car ambled past them, its purr briefly cracking the silence. A tune carried through an open window as someone sizzled a savoury dish in their pan.

When they neared the shrubs where Aileen had hidden the previous day, she pointed to the spot. 'Callan had parked his car here.'

Isla crouched in the meagre space. 'Cosy, well hidden… Where did you see the woman?'

Aileen settled next to her. They jostled until a few twigs

poked her back. It would be awkward if someone saw two grown women squatting in the hedges.

Squinting, she searched for the house the woman had stepped out from. The small cottages were so identical, she had trouble telling them apart at first.

She shut her eyes and focused her thoughts. 'The one with dry hedges. The penultimate one before the road turns left. That's the one.'

Isla studied it. 'You sure?'

'Yup. She got in the car, and he immediately took the turn. They didn't idle for long at the kerb.' Aileen uncurled, groaning as another twig nicked her neck.

Isla dusted her knees and stood. 'Come on.'

They strode towards the house with a single-minded focus.

The weeds and bushes in the yard were dry and haphazard, while dark spots on the walls spoke of years of neglect. The shut windows, with their drawn curtains, kept spying eyes at bay.

'Isla?' Aileen spoke in hushed tones. 'It looks abandoned.'

Isla narrowed her eyes. 'Appearances can be deceptive. Or it's someone who likes to draw their curtains and hates gardening.'

They hobbled towards the gate. It seemed unlikely someone could've been living there. The cobbled pathway to the front door had missing stones, and weeds jutted out all over the place.

And the front door? The colour had faded to a mucky brown with no signs of a number plate except for a faint outline.

The former residents had locked up; the brass door-knob sat blackened with age.

Tilting to the right, Aileen squinted through the netted

curtains. When they'd once been off white, they were now yellowish with age.

'Looks like someone left and never returned.'

Isla tapped her chin before peering at the abandoned street. 'What business did she have here?'

Aileen didn't know. 'Say, Isla, would you know who lived here?'

She shook her head but clicked her fingers. 'Aileen, you know this delivery we've to make?'

Aileen stopped her assessment of the cottage and frowned. 'What delivery?'

'Oh, you know, *the delivery*? This house could be the one we're looking for.' Grabbing Aileen's hand, Isla dragged her towards the unkempt house. 'Nosy neighbours!' She hissed under her breath.

Isla didn't look through the peephole in the door. Instead, she headed for the window to the right and peered in. 'Everything's covered up.'

Aileen tugged at her hair. The police could throw them behind bars for this…

She cupped her shaky hands on the dusty window and stuck her eyes in between her fingers. The building stank of moss and mortar.

The overcast sky and the murky window made it hard to see clearly. Aileen squinted, seeing a bare room with some furniture covered in white sheets.

Were the former residents moving back in? Whose house could this be?

The house belonged to a museum with stripped wallpaper from the 1990s and a huge radio with an antenna.

Emboldened, Aileen tugged at Isla's arm. 'Let's look through the back windows.'

The yard had tall prickly shrubs hiding Aileen and Isla from view.

Weeds had broken through the cobblestones here too, and a few stones wobbled.

'Careful!'

Aileen hoped they didn't sprain an ankle as they made their way to the back where, like the front, bushes and grass grew rampant.

A back door stood in the centre, with two windows either side.

They pressed their noses to the dusty window.

This room sat bare except for a wooden armoire similar to the one Aileen's gran had. An old box, a TV set, sat on it. Floral patterns bloomed on the wallpaper.

'It's ancient.'

'What's ancient?' a cold voice sneered, jolting them from their felonious activity.

Aileen jumped and stared into the eyes of the woman she'd seen yesterday. Her hair braided in perfect cornrows, her sharp eyes studied Aileen. They softened as they turned to Isla.

Isla chuckled nervously. 'Fayola, what a surprise!'

Fayola waved her hands to indicate their surroundings. 'I would say it's strange to find you in an empty backyard. At least I deal with a real estate like this.' Isla's eyes lit up. 'Are you selling this house?'

Fayola shot her a glare. 'I don't see how that's your business.'

Aileen licked her lips, fear clawing at her gut. She stared between Fayola and Isla.

Isla pulled out her packet of shortbread. 'I got an order to deliver these. The directions were so messed up, we're hopelessly lost. I'm sure we're searching for this address, although, like you pointed out, it's empty.'

'Unless there's a ghost in this house, desperate for your buttery biscuits,' Fayola said flippantly.

'Shortbread,' Isla hissed. 'It's shortbread.'

Fayola wasn't buying it. At six feet tall, she towered over their petite figures. With her hands folded and eyes glinting, she looked like an angry goddess.

Aileen swallowed to wet her throat and speak up, but Fayola beat her to it. 'Did Callan send *you* after the fiasco with Ms Willoughby?'

'Excuse me?' Aileen gaped at the woman. 'I'm not here with the police, nor with Callan. We're here to deliver shortbread. Now, if this is the wrong address' – Aileen pulled Isla by the wrist – 'we're leaving!'

Before they could round the house, Fayola snapped back, 'If Callan has the guts, ask him to come and speak with me. Next time I find you loitering about, I'll report you for trespassing!'

'How rude!' Aileen scowled as they made their way back to the bakery.

Isla huffed. 'She's usually so friendly when she comes to buy her gluten-free bread each morning.'

'Who was she?'

Isla explained Fayola Noah used to be an estate agent until she retired the year before. And as Hailey Noah's mother and Adelaide's wife, her involvement made things murky.

'Is Hailey Noah a friend of Callan's?'

'Hailey should be friends with Daniel too. They're of the same age and there's only one school in town. At best, they must be acquaintances.'

Aileen parked the car in the market square and the two of them hiked towards the bakery when Isla halted mid-step. 'Hey, why don't we ask Daniel about these dynamics? He'll know! I have to pick Carly up from him, anyway.'

To kill two birds with one stone, they hiked two doors down to Daniel's shop.

Hopefully, he could provide some answers.

❄

Callan barely had the energy to get ready for the day. For the first time, he trudged towards his office, five minutes late for his shift, wearing a sullen face and in no hurry to get behind his desk.

Rory was on the phone, the door to his office open, but unlike every other morning, he didn't send a wave Callan's way.

Officer Robert Davis wasn't at his desk. He must be on an errand or solving the case which should've been his.

A bittersweet cloak settled on his tongue.

Callan eyed the piles of paper littering his desk. He should clean his office. An ambitious goal, it seemed, although he had ample time now. No more racking his brain over Blaine's case.

He picked up the first pile and groaned. Coffee could help smooth things over.

❄

The coffee left a bitter zing in his mouth yet put no dent in the filing. He sat on the floor, all the papers from his desk scattered around him. They would drown him, just like his thoughts. The files on his desk hadn't thinned, the wooden top of his desk way out of sight.

The papers crackled as Callan attacked them, trying to keep his mind several paces away from what had happened yesterday. He'd stayed up half the night, replaying every wee moment of his afternoon. No more.

Rory's voice drifted into his office. 'Aye, I understand… Aye…'

Callan tuned him out. It might be a wee bit childish, but he was furious with his boss.

Several silent minutes later, Callan muttered a curse and stared at his bloodied thumb. When humans didn't cut into him, paper did.

He sucked the blood off his finger and heard someone chuckle from the doorway. 'Um, I wasn't expecting ye to be sitting on the floor on yer arse sucking yer thumb. Should I —' The glare Callan sent his way shut down the officer's babble.

'What do ye want, Robert?'

'Oh, what should I do with this?' He held up an evidence bag. It contained a black jacket. The light in Callan's room caught the metallic zipper and the leather finish.

'What's that?'

Robert cleared his throat. 'The evidence found in the street next to Ms Willoughby's house.'

Callan froze. Why had Robert brought the evidence to him?

'Officer Davis!' Rory called from his office. 'Didn't I ask ye to bring the evidence to me?'

Robert flinched, yet his twinkling eyes met Callan's. Had the green-as-meadows officer just supplied him with a clue?

Judging by the small smirk playing on his lips, he had.

'Ouch.' Callan looked at his ring finger this time. Another paper cut.

Bloody hell! To hell with the papers.

Callan piled them all together and dumped them onto his desk again. He didn't want to file. Papers would hardly help him. They just irked him.

A black leather jacket in a side alley. Who owned it?

How could they know it belonged to the bastard who'd hurt Ms Willoughby? Did they have witnesses?

Callan wished he could investigate. He could help—

The phone's shrill ringing halted those hopeful thoughts.

No, Rory wanted him far away from this case. In the five years he'd worked under him, he'd never been this aggressive. If for nothing else, Callan wouldn't push Rory because he respected the man. Boss or not, he owed Rory a lot.

Callan pulled out his phone and pressed it to his ear. 'Hello?'

'Callan! Get here at once,' the person hissed and hung up.

No name, no address. Well, Callan growled, he knew who it was: a furry cat's annoying owner.

❄

A SENSE OF DÉJÀ VU SET IN AS CALLAN DROVE INTO THE neighbourhood. Yesterday, a visit to a similar setting had flipped his world on its head. Some houses had picket fences; others had small stone walls, but in all the yards bloomed clusters of plants bursting with flowers.

A lady, her greying hair glinting under the sun, hunched over a bush. An apron protected the front of her skirt. She hummed as she worked.

No one loitered about. In the five-minute hike from where he'd parked in the designated area to Mrs Douglas's house, no one drove or walked past him.

The older populace of Loch Fuar called this neighbourhood home. They had a committee, which made it easy for members to get access to volunteers who'd help with chores.

Callan could walk to Mrs Douglas's house in his sleep, considering how often she called him. Despite his annoyance at the old woman, Rory had urged him to entertain her.

She had only her fluffy cat for company. As far as humans went, Callan was her sole visitor. He couldn't imagine why.

The metallic gate slammed shut behind him. The thing protested like an unoiled machine and a bird squawked in protest.

Callan swatted a stray bead of sweat from his forehead and blinked at the scorching sun. Where had the storm gone?

The sweet smell of roses tickled his nostrils. Mrs Douglas spent a lot of time in her garden, too. She had numerous varieties of flora and took great pleasure in showing them off. He'd spent an agonising day following her as she explained every plant, flower, and leaf in her garden.

Steeling himself, he knocked on her door twice, not wanting to hear her weird chiming doorbell, and stood back.

It took her thirty foot taps to answer.

The strong sweet-smelling aroma of tea and cookies hit him like a tsunami, followed by an angry *meow*!

Seventy-year-old Mrs Douglas had flushed plump cheeks, a sign she'd fumed at her neighbour. She gestured vividly, hitting Callan in the face. 'Warren, that insufferable man. He's putting a fence in my garden!'

Callan sighed. Warren was a retired lieutenant general. Since he'd moved here twenty years ago, he and Mrs Douglas had never seen eye to eye.

If he were in Warren's shoes, he'd have built a fence a long time ago.

Unlike his emotionless features and close-cropped hair, Warren loved cultivating a vegetable patch in his backyard no matter the hard work, especially since he did it all himself.

Mrs Douglas's fluffy cat didn't give two hoots. He used Warren's patch as his private mud-bathing-tub-cum-toilet.

Callan sometimes thought the cat did it on purpose and wore a smug smile every time Callan had to return him to his mistress.

'Ask him to stop!' Mrs Douglas's shriek echoed through the neighbourhood.

Callan huffed and pulled out his notepad. Half the paperwork in his office belonged to this woman and her hundred complaints.

It at least kept him employed.

An hour later, he'd calmed Mrs Douglas and paid a visit to Warren to enquire about the fence.

The man had his original house plans ready and showed Callan where the fence would go. He also pointed out a small shed in his backyard where he stored his tools. He'd attached a special lock to it so Mrs Douglas's cat wouldn't break into his sack of fertilisers.

Callan had taken the plans to Mrs Douglas and told her Warren wasn't pitching his fence on her land.

A brief face-off had ensued, punctuated by the cat's constant hissing.

Now feeling like he'd worked forty-eight hours non-stop, Callan rubbed his forehead as Mrs Douglas's creaking gate shut behind him.

From homicide, Rory had demoted him to babysitting elderlies.

That's what you get for messing up a case, Cameron!

A hit of real coffee from Isla's Bakery would be the

perfect fix, especially considering he had more than half of his shift to get through.

And it promised to be a long one for sure.

Callan strode towards his car when a burly figure turned the corner. The man's muscles strained against his thin tank top, shimmering under the sun's heat. Damp, shoulder-length hair fell into his eyes. Who walked the streets in a dirt-green tank top dripping with sweat like a pig?

The gym sat on the other side of town, along with a small tattoo parlour. This man obviously frequented both.

And unfortunately, Callan recognised him: Cosimo Bocelli.

'Hey, Callan! What's up?' He sounded surprised and grinned like a loony.

Callan halted mid-step, contemplating crossing the road. He'd gone looking for Cosimo yesterday, hadn't he? He could strike up a harmless conversation, surely? So what if it gave him insight into a case Rory had dismissed him from?

He narrowed his eyes, giving Cosimo a once-over. Mud coated his knees and the hem of his trousers. And judging by the splotches of brown on his sweat-coated forehead, the man had been working in mud, perhaps volunteering for a senior member of their community.

Cosimo volunteered? Callan had known little about Cosimo until a couple of days ago – since learning he'd been the last person to see Blaine before he disappeared, Callan had done a background check on him.

Unemployed despite his sound engineering degree, Cosimo didn't have the best track record with jobs, possibly because he liked to visit the pub a bit too often, though his experience with the ladies had apparently given him a smooth tongue.

'Hey, I heard ye're looking at Blaine's case again.' He jumped right to it, his foolish grin tempering to a grimace.

Callan cleared his throat. Well, *he* hadn't broached the topic. Technically, he hadn't disobeyed his boss. 'Aye, the *police* are looking into his case again.'

Cosimo whistled, running a hand through his soggy hair. 'Fifteen years, eh? I thought he'd be a David Bowie by now.'

'Piano,' Callan managed. How had Blaine considered this eejit a friend when he didn't remember what talents the lad had had?

Cosimo blinked, clearly confused. 'What?'

Callan's voice sounded like a whip. 'Blaine played the piano. He wasn't into singing. Hated it, in fact.'

Cosimo shuffled his legs, clearly not caring for Callan's tone. 'Ah, aye. He played the keys. I remember now.'

Silence overtook their conversation, yet neither man attempted to move.

A bird's wail jolted them out of their reveries. Cosimo perked up. 'Hey, ye should come to the pub tonight. We'll invite Gerry and Jason. Some good fun with the lads, eh?'

Callan crossed his arms and, unusually, suppressed the flickers of temptation to say yes. Based on his theory, one of his former friends had lied, especially about their camping trip. It would be torture hanging out with them.

'I can't. I'm on duty tonight.'

'Blast! It would've been fun to catch up, eh?' A grin erupted on Cosimo's face again, as if they hadn't just been discussing their missing friend.

Callan dipped his hands in his pockets. 'Say, do ye remember the last time ye saw him?'

Cosimo stared off into the distance and wobbled on his feet. A car whizzed past them, hooting a greeting. Cosimo waved. 'Let me think… In school? In class?' Wiggling his fingers, Cosimo turned back to Callan. 'Aye, I saw him in class. The smarty pants had earned an A, and I'd failed. Remember it now.'

It didn't corroborate Patricia's statement or Rory's notes. Callan folded his hands and spread his legs. 'Not on yer date?'

The eejit's eyebrows shot into his hair. 'Date?'

'Aye, the one with Patricia.'

Cosimo was at sea, judging by the glassy look in his eyes. Had he gone off on so many dates he couldn't remember one from the other?

According to Jason, he had a good memory. You needed one if you were juggling various girlfriends at once.

Cosimo clicked his fingers. 'Oh, the date with Patricia. We were by the…' He trailed off.

When Cosimo swirled his forefinger, as if the answer would come to him with some magic of his fingers, Callan offered, 'Loch?'

'Loch, aye! Patricia and me by the loch. Couldn't remember it well – still can't. Hey, are ye going to arrest me now?' He chuckled nervously.

Callan unfolded his arms, holding up a hand. 'No, not going to arrest ye. If ye remember anything else, ye can reach DCI Rory Macdonald at the station. The police would appreciate yer help.'

Cosimo clicked his feet on the footpath. 'Sure will! Now I've got to dash. I'm late!' He hurried off, shouting the last bit over his shoulders.

The man was so disorganised. Callan snorted, hoping to rid himself of the acrid stench of sweat he'd left behind.

Coffee. Isla's aromatic brew with a lemon tart would salvage the day.

CHAPTER SIX

The wind blew up a riot as tourists queued behind the ice-cream van. Trees swayed and the sun, a bright orange ball, ignited against glass windows.

Isla pulled the door open to Daniel's shop and gestured for Aileen to hurry. Both women sighed upon entering the cool air-conditioned space.

Heat waves were the worst!

Aileen wetted her dry lips as Daniel came around the counter. 'Aileen! Oh, sweetheart!' his gruff voice boomed. 'What a surprise.'

Isla strutted over to her husband. 'Carly?'

'Playing with her toys.' Daniel pointed to the back room. 'I thought ye'd be here after the lunch crowd settled.'

Isla flung her arms around his neck and hugged him tight. Aileen watched in awe as a small smile tickled his lips and he bent lower to hug his wife tighter.

Isla's voice sounded muffled against Daniel's shirt. 'Oh, you are never going to believe the day we've had!'

Daniel stroked her back.

How exciting would it be to have such trust? Their love and synergy crafted an unbreakable bond. Aileen's heart zinged.

She shuffled her legs when Isla straightened from their embrace and pecked Daniel on his lips. 'So, Aileen was following a man.'

His eyebrows shot up in alarm. 'She— What?'

Daniel and Callan had the occasional lads' night out. Would Daniel rat her out? She didn't need Callan's reprimand. Although he'd have to speak to her then.

Isla stroked Daniel's back in gentle circles. 'Nothing dangerous! Just satisfying our curiosity.' And she recounted their hike to Wallace Street and running into Fayola.

When her story ended, Daniel frowned. 'Are ye sure ye went to *that* house?'

Aileen and Isla shared a look. Why did he say it like that?

He glanced at the back room, running a hand through his hair. 'It's… Blaine Macgregor lived there.'

The air conditioners stopped buzzing. Aileen's heart picked up its pace and she gaped.

They'd been to the missing lad's house?

Daniel sank into a chair behind the counter. His broad shoulders drooped. 'The Macgregors moved in when we were about eleven or twelve. Callan and I, we struck up a friendship with Blaine. The lad had brains. It scared the bullies, it did, so they beat him up, played nasty pranks. We thought, being strapping lads, we could help, so we saw him home most days after school. There's no way I'd forget where he lived.'

Aileen let his words sink in, although it gave rise to more questions. How was Matthew Edgar connected to Blaine's house? Or had he been there as Fayola's friend?

'You said Fayola Noah's an estate agent, right?'

Isla bobbed her head. 'Do you think she's selling the house?'

They mulled over her question until a cloud masked the sunlight and the queue at the ice-cream van extended around the block.

She'd last visited Daniel's handyman shop when she'd wanted to fix a leaky roof and had poked a hole in the ceiling.

Aileen grimaced at her former naïve self. Daniel had been so helpful back when she'd moved to Loch Fuar in March. Months later, she still hadn't learned to wield a hammer.

Daniel stood, his chair scraping against the tiled floor. His muscular six-foot-three frame filled the space. 'Who'd ask her to sell? Aileen, ye said this man picked Fayola up in front of the house. Chances are they're acquaintances, and she met him there. Adelaide Noah, her wife, has a shop not far from Wallace Street.'

'That can't be. I saw her shut the door behind her and walk to Mr Edgar's car! I'm sure.'

Daniel frowned. 'Mr Edgar?'

'He's a guest at the inn – old, and he limps. From Inverness.'

Daniel didn't know any such man.

Isla leaned against the counter and crossed her legs at the ankles. 'Do you think she inspected the place for a potential buyer?'

'Who'd ask her to inspect it?'

Aileen didn't know. What she had were a few questions about the missing lad and Callan. 'Daniel, since you're the only person who could give us a background about the scene in Loch Fuar fifteen years ago—'

Isla rubbed her hands together. 'I don't know much

about your teenage years, either. What rebellious things did you do?'

Daniel ran a hand through his golden-brown locks, a blush blooming on his face. It had to be a wee bit embarrassing telling your wife what shenanigans you got up to as a teen. 'I didn't. I mean, I'd never be reckless or anything!'

The poor man. The blush and shy look in his eyes had Isla's gaze softening.

'I don't mind if you were, sweetheart. Why don't you tell us about your friends and their secrets?' Her eyes twinkled with a brutal glint. Isla had slipped from wife mode to gossipmonger.

Daniel pushed his hands into his pockets, spluttered, and then steadied himself. 'Callan and I, we've been best buds since forever. But ye ken how those awkward years are – we change and things around us change.'

Aileen scribbled down what Daniel said, a journalist crafting her report. 'What do you mean by "things around us change"?'

Daniel shuffled his legs and shot Isla a nervous glance before setting his eyes firmly on Aileen's. 'Callan had plans. Wait, let me explain it from the beginning. About the time we hit thirteen, Callan and I didn't share any classes. We met occasionally to play football and the like, although we weren't inseparable like we once were.

'Blaine and I shared most classes. His father expected straight As, which he scored every term. We partnered on a couple of projects and studied together, and I introduced Blaine to Callan. The three of us would hang out.'

When Daniel trailed off, eyes on the floor, Isla nudged him. 'What happened next?'

Aileen leaned against the doorframe and let the sunlight warm her neck.

Daniel took his time to respond. 'Callan and Blaine,

they wanted to leave Loch Fuar behind, as did Gerald Erwin, Patricia Adair, Cosimo Bocelli, Hailey Noah and Jason Mitso. I don't know how they bonded – none of them were anything alike. They called themselves the "White Birds" or some such name.'

Daniel straightened. 'Ye ken how people create groups at that age. They stick to the same set of friends. Me? I didn't belong to one; nor did I want to leave.'

Isla swatted a hand, dismissing Daniel's melancholy. 'He's being humble. Dan got straight As too, and this revered institute chose him for a course taken by the crème de la crème. Was it to do with physics or maths, love?'

Her husband grumbled. Aileen would've never pegged the handyman as a studious person.

'Both. I had a full scholarship, but my instinct said I should stay. So I turned to the vocation I knew best.' He pointed around his shop. 'I can lose myself in fixing a leak as easily as I can in books. It turns out my gut's got the best compass ever.' He sent the sweetest smile Isla's way.

Would Callan ever look at her like Daniel did Isla? Aileen jolted, caught unawares by such a ludicrous thought. She shook herself and bit her lip when a blush crept into Isla's cheeks.

Goodness, did this *thing* make everyone tipsy?

Isla grinned. 'If he hadn't stayed back, we'd have never met. I'd be nowhere close to Glasgow or university.' She shuddered. 'I considered it lucky when I passed.'

'Not in cooking class, for sure.' Daniel patted his belly. The grin promptly vanished from his face. 'Now ye ken what Loch Fuar's teenaged populace had been up to. I don't ken about now. This town ye see today? It's far more advanced than twenty years ago.'

The 'White Birds' consisted of ambitious people, and Aileen had experience with such folks. That experience had taught her that most ambitious people would do anything to achieve their goal. 'Did all the members of this White Birds group leave?'

Daniel chuckled dryly. 'We all thought Blaine got away finally.' A sombre shadow fell across his face. 'Callan left for a while. And of course, Gerald Erwin left for medical school. He returned after graduation to take over from his father. I dinnae ken about the rest, although they're all here now.'

'Dr Erwin's father practised medicine?'

'Of course – Gerald comes from a family of doctors. He must be the tenth generation or so.'

Aileen hadn't known. She scrawled it all in her notes, a plan forming in her mind.

Isla, hands on her hips, stared back and forth between Aileen and Daniel. When they both fell silent, she asked, 'Where does this info lead us?'

She didn't know yet. 'Knowledge is power. And if Fayola Noah's selling Blaine's house, someone's set her to the job.'

Tapping her chin, Isla asked, 'Where do the Macgregors stay now?'

'They moved out of town, sweetheart.'

Aileen flipped her notepad closed, mind chugging through the information she had. Their next course of action: brainstorm. It wouldn't be the same without Callan, although Isla had the smarts.

She gestured to her friend. 'Come on – we need some thinking time and lemonade.'

❄

Callan scowled at Isla's absence. She never ditched her bakery.

A go-cup filled with iced coffee and a paper bag with his lemon tart sat on the counter. The change clattered next to it.

Isla's red-haired nephew, Andrew, worked hard. Callan pegged him as a decent lad.

'Where's Isla?' Callan had his suspicions, and he wanted to know if they were true.

Andrew shrugged. 'She left with Ms Aileen a while ago.'

Ah, so he'd hit the nail on the head. Those two were trouble, especially when paired.

He thanked Andrew and strode out of the bakery. They wouldn't get into unnecessary problems. Aileen had shown little interest in this case, even after finding Candace Willoughby in his car. Usually she would pester him till he told her everything he knew.

Callan sipped his iced coffee, and his entire body ignited with new life. Gosh, he'd needed this.

Reaching inside the paper bag, his eyes latched onto a white van parked in the alley. It had the words 'Adelaide's Arty World' painted in hot pink curly cursive.

Adelaide Noah, Hailey's mother, had to be out making deliveries at the post office as per her daily ritual.

He'd have never crossed paths with her usually, but today Callan set his eyes on the mission.

The chain they'd found around Candace's wrists might've been his. Yet when it should've shown its age, it gleamed.

The cold liquid of the coffee soothed his stomach. He needed to be calm when speaking to Adelaide.

He headed towards the post office that lay beyond Barbara's Tea Room. Thanks to the late afternoon hour, the tea room bustled with customers. Most late afternoons were meant to enjoy a blether, and the sweltering heat made Barbara's the perfect place.

Most of the customers huddled inside were gossiping about the case, he was sure of it. The disappearance of a teenager had taken the town's gossip wheel in a flurry fifteen years ago, and it would today as well.

Loitering by the post office, Callan studied its navy-blue door. It lurched ajar by an inch. The elderly Sam Walker didn't sit sentinel behind the desk as usual.

Hoping to last outside a wee bit longer, Callan savoured the icy, bitter residue of the coffee on his tongue. He bit into the tangy-sweet tart for want of sugary heaven and enjoyed the contrasting textures it offered.

He'd swallowed the last morsel when Adelaide stepped out. Her brown hair fell to her shoulders, her body hunched as if she didn't want to be noticed.

What did she have to hide? Callan narrowed his eyes, studying her retreating back.

Her oversized purple dress gave her the appearance of a skeleton with skin.

She didn't notice him, yet she'd contorted her bony face in a scowl. Had she always been this way? Callan remembered a woman who'd invited him and his friends into her home with open arms. No, she'd turned sour when he'd pinned his new badge to his belt.

'Mrs Noah?' he called after her and braced himself at the same moment.

She halted, swivelled, and her scowl deepened. 'Aye?'

Callan came to a halt a few feet away, not wanting to come within shooting range. 'Would ye help me out for a moment?'

'Is this about the investigation?' Her eyes narrowed, and she shot him a glare. 'I've got nothing to do with Blaine Macgregor. Neither does Hailey. Leave us out of it!'

What did she have against police officers? Most people would be happy to be questioned by the police – especially the gossipmongers. It made them the centre of attention.

The wind picked up speed, tugging at Callan's empty paper bag.

'I want to know about a chain. Ye probably crafted it as a commission for someone.'

Adelaide lifted her chin. 'Some commissions are confidential. Ye'll need a warrant.'

Warrant? He didn't need a bloody warrant. He needed answers, especially since he couldn't solve this case officially.

He'd stick to the rules. 'Look, I'm not asking ye in an official capacity. Blaine's a friend so I… I'm not investigating his disappearance.'

Adelaide scoffed. 'Why are ye bothering me? After what ye did to Candace Willoughby, I'm surprised Rory's still kept ye on his team!'

That hurt, thinking… knowing everyone thought him an abuser of women. They couldn't be more wrong. 'Did someone commission a pendant shaped like a bird in the past year?'

She stared for a while, as if thinking about what to say. 'No.'

Callan thrust his hand in his pocket. The other gripped his takeaway bag. 'In the last year, hasn't anyone from Loch Fuar commissioned a necklace or chain?'

Adelaide sighed. 'I've done a lot of work this past year. I couldn't recollect. Ye could visit me at my shop. I have a list somewhere. Or ye could ask Hailey. Now, if ye're done, I've got to get going. I've got a few more deliveries to make.'

'Thank ye. I—' He huffed. Adelaide had jogged off.

He was trudging towards his office when his phone

vibrated in his pocket. It had been ringing a lot today. His family had got wind of the situation. His mother had even insisted she'd come and speak with Rory on his behalf. Was he in bloody nursery and needed his maw to speak with the teacher?

Bloody hell! For his mother, he just might be.

Callan pushed the front door of the police station a bit too harshly. It protested, the sound echoing in the space.

Behind the front desk, Robert gave him a half-hearted smile. 'Is that coffee? Ye'll need it.'

The door to Rory's office clicked and out stepped an old man. His thinning hair had left him bald except for a stray hair or two above his ears. He wore a plaid shirt, coupled with a grim expression.

Without a word to Callan, he stalked off.

Another one of his non-admirers.

'My office, Cameron. Now!' Rory called.

Callan dumped the paper bag and go-cup in the dustbin and plodded to his boss's office. Robert's gaze followed him all the way.

For the second time in a week, Callan took a seat in Rory's neat space.

Rory steepled his fingers and sent him a glare cold enough to freeze the world over. 'I want to inform ye the Willoughbys are corresponding with the Citizens Advice Bureau to draft a complaint against yer conduct.'

Callan shut his eyes. His decade of service, from a rookie on the streets to the high-profile cases he'd dealt with before moving back to Loch Fuar, flashed in front of his eyes. Had all those long hours and vicious nightmares led to this?

His boss didn't sympathise. 'They'll send the complaint to the Professional Standards Department as ye ken.'

And the PSD would send an officer to investigate. He

knew it all – had seen it unfold for a fellow officer once. Hell, he'd made DCI Kevin Roland lumber through this same process, hadn't he?

Rubbing his eyes did nothing to ease the strain behind them. Callan's shoulders bunched up to his ears. 'I didn't do it, Rory.'

Rory's chair scraped across the floor. 'Someone has brutally assaulted a frail 87-year-old woman. She's got bruises on her wrists and marks on her neck! The chain dug into her wrists. Since last night, she's been hysterical in the hospital. And all ye have to say is ye didn't do it?'

Not knowing what else to say, Callan hung his head. He hadn't hurt her. An idea came to his mind. 'The jacket Robert found—'

'Looks very similar to yours,' Rory barked, his face set in an unreadable mask. 'It looks bad for ye.'

Callan's shoulders drooped and his head throbbed like someone had hammered a thousand nails into it.

'Decades on this force, decades and never once has anyone questioned the integrity of my department. I always do things by the book and encourage my officers to do so too.'

He strode over to Callan's side. Placing a hand on the desk, Rory loomed over the younger man. 'I never thought the PSD would investigate my detectives, let alone you.'

Callan met his boss's angry eyes. They held contempt in them also – contempt fused with disappointment. And the disappointment crushed Callan.

Yes, this debacle had flushed his decade of loyal service down the drain, along with the respect his boss had for him. Which hurt the most? Callan couldn't tell.

CHAPTER SEVEN

Isla hummed and sat back in the chair. They'd brought Carly along to the bakery, and after Isla had instructed her two part-time employees to manage the crowds, they'd slipped into her office.

Andrew informed them of Callan's visit. Aileen rolled her eyes.

Talk about mixed signals.

Now a handful of chocolate wrappers were scattered across the table, and Aileen's notepad lay open to the notes she'd taken.

'Let's head to Hailey Noah's. What do you say? She was Blaine's friend, wasn't she?'

Aileen scoffed. 'We can't just barge into her house and question her!'

Isla swatted the air, apparently at ease with strutting into a stranger's house. 'She's a regular at the bakery, and we talk often. She won't mind.'

❄

Aileen turned into the parking area for Adelaide's Arty World after dropping a slumbering Carly back at Daniel's – Isla didn't want to talk about Daniel's former friends in front of her wee one, and Daniel was over the moon to get his bairn back so he could ooh and ah at her. According to Isla, he hogged their child's attention.

The afternoon was fresh with the earthy fragrance that lingered after a shower. It had drizzled for a couple of minutes, cooling the heated soil. Birds sang, and the sun was at a pleasant angle.

They walked over to the shop as the front door opened and Hailey emerged.

Isla gestured to Aileen, and the two of them skirted the stone cottage and headed for the backyard.

Hailey leaned against the window on her side of the cottage, smoking a cigarette.

The acrid smell of tobacco assaulted Aileen's nostrils. She twisted her nose.

Seeing her contorted face, Hailey chuckled. 'Sorry. It's been hectic.' She threw the cigarette on the gravel and stubbed it out with a booted foot.

Aileen exchanged a quick glance with Isla. 'What's been bothering you?' Isla ventured.

Hailey twirled a bony hand. 'Ye name it. My mothers had a terrible row, there's this jewellery I've got to get done and that missing person case has brought my past up when all I want is to forget it!'

Nobody wanted to dig up their wonder years – too often, they weren't all that wonderful.

'Parents can be a handful.'

Hailey leaned forward and gave Aileen a once-over. 'What brings ye by? Don't get me wrong, I love having ye here, but I've heard of yer penchant for solving cases. Are ye looking into Blaine's disappearance?'

Aileen bit her lip. 'Not really. We just wanted to know about Blaine.'

A bird cooed, hidden among the trees. The leaves rustled in the breeze and played through Aileen's loose hair.

Hailey shrugged it off, a gesture she seemed to do often, and leaned against the wall again.

'Like any teens, we had big dreams. I didn't pursue mine. There was never the right time. My mother, Adelaide – she fell sick the same summer Blaine went missing, and I didn't want to leave mum alone. Mum's Fayola; I call Adelaide "Mama". So I lost touch with the rest of the group. My goals didn't match theirs. White Birds we were, about to take flight and colour those bare wings.'

Aileen jotted it all down. 'When was this? You losing touch?'

'I was seventeen or eighteen. Right when Blaine disappeared. He was a kind boy and helped me with my studies. He'd offer to help with the dishes and such when he'd come over. Good lad now lost…'

Aileen tilted her head. 'What about the rest of your friends?'

Hailey snorted. 'Nasty. I was glad I left them. They were toxic friendships, not relationships which surpassed our joint goal of moving away. Callan was a personable lad, although he had his own troubles.'

Aileen frowned. What troubles could Callan have at eighteen?

He hadn't told her a word. In fact, they hadn't communicated properly for days now. Not since he'd dropped her off at Dachaigh, cracking her up with his silly jokes. The carefree side of Callan had disappeared, as if he'd never existed.

And here she'd thought he brought out his playful side for her.

Aileen didn't want to know about his troubles from Hailey or anyone else. She wanted to hear them from the horse's mouth… if he ever spoke to her again.

She grinned at Hailey. 'Thank you so much for helping us out.'

They walked back to the car, lost in thought, when a white van pulled into the driveway. A bone-thin woman hopped out and slammed the door so hard, the van rattled.

Striding up the driveway, she yelled. 'Bloody Fayola! What does she think—'

As if just noticing Aileen and Isla, she stopped short. Isla bobbed her head. 'Adelaide.'

Adelaide flicked her wavy brown hair and hurried inside.

The chime sounded, signalling the door clicking in place.

'Wow, rude much?'

Isla took Aileen by the arm. 'She's short-tempered. Come on, she's left enough space for us to reverse out of here.'

'Well, she suits Fayola alright.'

Isla rounded the car and slipped in. 'Fayola doesn't hang around the shop, not unless she wants something from Adelaide. A little bird tells me there's trouble in marital paradise and has been for quite some time.'

'Oh?' Aileen drawled.

Small town and its accurate gossip never failed to amuse her. And unlike the tabloids, it never had to brew eye-catching news. The town's residents scandalised their neighbourhood out of boredom.

The car purred to life. 'Who can we speak to next?'

Isla grinned at her, her mind busy scheming. 'Patricia!'

It took them until after dusk to get to Patricia's. Carly needed a cuddle with her mum, and Aileen's car ran low on petrol, so they switched to Isla's. If someone saw Isla's car outside Patricia's house, it wouldn't be too suspicious considering they were friends.

When the birds called it a day, Isla parked in the lane adjacent to Patricia's cottage. Patricia's electrician's shop sat below the living area, but it was only half as big as Adelaide and Fayola's store.

Ivy hugged the beige stone walls and rustled with the wind. Beside Aileen, Isla sighed. 'Looks like a rainy night.'

Aileen peeked at the darkening sky and found grey clouds lurking.

Despite the late hour, they peeked inside the shop first. Isla shook her head. 'Funny. I had Patricia pegged as a workaholic. I've never seen her close shop unless she's out running errands.'

But everything was silent and dark. Sockets, wires, boxes and various tools Aileen couldn't name littered a wooden shelf, while a stack of files sat on a shelf against the back wall.

The tall blond woman who owned the place was missing. Isla took Aileen's arm. 'Let's try upstairs.'

'I'm not sure we can do that, Isla.'

Impatiently, Isla tugged her forward. 'Come on!'

Crash!

The sound of glass smashing splintered the croaking of crickets. They both sank to the ground instantly.

What was happening?

A movement caught Aileen's eye. It was the room above the store. Where it had been in darkness before, it was now awash in a golden glow.

Patricia had drawn the creamy curtains, but the window framed two silhouettes – a man and a woman. They were facing each other, yet the way their hands moved and bodies stood rigid showed they were arguing.

Frozen, Aileen lifted a trembling hand to point the scene out. Isla had already seen it.

Aileen's breath tickled her lips. 'Who could it be?'

Isla too lowered her voice. It trembled with fear. 'Patricia, I'm sure of it, although it looks like—'

'Daniel?'

'Callan,' Isla finished at the same time.

'What?'

The chorus reached the couple upstairs, and suddenly there was a loud silence. The shadows shifted. Damn, they'd been spotted. Hopefully, their faces weren't visible crouched here in the dark! The last thing Aileen needed was a complaint to the police, aka DI Callan Cameron.

Aileen grasped Isla's hand and made a run for it.

They dashed out of Patricia's front yard and took the turn into the other alley. Everything was silent except for the breeze and their scampering feet. The mist sent chills slithering across Aileen's back. Yet she persisted.

Beside her, Isla huffed, her red hair bouncing behind her and her pants like the puffing of a steam engine.

No sooner had they left than a piercing scream filled the air. The scream brought Isla to a faltering standstill. It was so chilling, Aileen's steps stammered and she too skidded to a halt. 'Oh, gosh. Isla! Come on. Let's not wait here.'

'We can't run away. That man! He might hurt her.' Isla was panting, a hand over her heart, the other on her knees. The determination in her green eyes was unmissable.

'We'll call the police. We need backup!' Aileen reached for her phone.

Isla dismissed Aileen's plea and dragged her towards Patricia's flat again. 'There's one man and two of us. Come on!'

Not willing to send Isla off on her own, Aileen followed on tiptoe. They passed the stone wall, and Aileen chanced a glance at the window above. It was still lit, but no silhouettes stood there anymore.

Her palpitating heart resembled the insistent beat of a drum.

They made their way to the back, the path lit by the steady, eerie glow of the moon. If it hadn't been for Isla, Aileen would have quaked in her boots.

A narrow iron staircase stood behind the back door leading to the cottage's upper level. On its other side was a garbage bin. The rest of the yard was just dried-out grass – no pots or trees.

Patricia wasn't an avid gardener.

Careful to make less noise than a kitten, Isla took the stairs first. Aileen brought up the rear, watching to see if there was anyone lurking in the shadows.

'Oh!' Isla's gasp made Aileen jump.

'What? What is it?'

'The door's open.'

She pushed it with one hand, and it let out a loud creak.

Aileen's heart was about to beat out of her chest. Her hands were clammy and her body braced.

She could do this! Callan had taught her how to defend herself. *Damn that oaf!*

Following Isla inside, she exhaled. 'Oh crap.'

The furniture in the room was all destroyed. On the floor lay cushions, ornaments, boxes and other items, sprawled as if a tornado had spirited through the room.

The stuffy space was heavy with the stench of malt,

and a flowery perfume mingled with an acrid, gut-churning stench.

The kitchen was in a similar state. Someone had pulled out utensils and drawers, and a few pieces of broken china littered the floor.

The overturned bin emitted a pungent odour which was hard to ignore.

A tiny whimper brought their attention to the last door at the end of the corridor. It was wide open and revealed a single bed covered with white linens.

Isla made a dash for it, Aileen in tow. To make sure the man wasn't still in the house, Aileen checked the bathroom. She found the toiletries and towels thrown on the grimy floor.

Another whimper brought her attention back to the bedroom. Patricia lay on the floor below the window where she'd stood just a few minutes ago.

A trickle of blood ran from her forearm to her wrists, and she whimpered.

Isla crouched beside her. 'Patricia! Patricia. It's okay. It's Aileen and me.'

They helped her sit on the bed. Bent at a forty-five-degree angle, Aileen noticed the state of the mattress. A long, sinister gash split it open. And in the centre of the bed was a long kitchen knife, an Excalibur of doom.

Swallowing a lump of trepidation, Aileen brought a chair over from the dining area.

Patricia slouched, never meeting their gaze. Isla's mothering tendencies took over. 'Where's your first aid kit? We need to get your wound bandaged. And then I'll take you to the hospital.'

As if slapped out of her trance, Patricia's gaze flittered between them. 'Isla? Aileen? What are you doing here? Get out! Get out!' She shoved at them.

Isla was having none of it. 'You're injured. Let me take you to the doctor. Aileen'll call the police.'

'Police! No.' Patricia struggled, pushing Isla's helpful hands away. 'I don't want to go to the doctor's; nor do I want the police here. I want nothing to do with them. Go away.'

'Please, Patricia. Let us help you.'

Now her voice, shrill with panic, boomed through the room. 'Calling the police will do me no good. They can't protect me. They'll never find a fault with him. Leave me alone. Please. He might kill me otherwise.'

Aileen lowered herself to Patricia's eye level. 'Who?'

She shook her head. 'Leave before your life is under threat too.'

❄

Callan swiped a hand over his forehead. The air conditioning droning above his head had given him a nagging headache.

In the last few hours, he'd put a small dent in the ever-growing papers scattered in his office.

Callan had found a bureau of drawers buried in one corner of his office, under files and heaps of loose papers.

Taking Aileen's advice, he'd brought out a stapler and punch and done his best imitation of her, carefully straightening the papers and arranging them in categories.

If she saw him now, sat on the floor filing, he bet she'd get a kick.

Aileen…

His heart clenched.

No, it was good riddance. She hadn't contacted him, except for those brief phone calls and messages she'd dropped after Rory had taken him off the case.

She'd made no attempts to meet him or… Goodness, he sounded like a pompous prick.

Callan placed his palm over his right knee and stared at his prosthetic leg.

She hadn't commented on it – ever. She'd been curious, like she was about most things, but unlike Patricia, Aileen hadn't scorned him over his disability once since she'd found out about it.

And they'd been in numerous situations together – life-threatening situations where she'd had ample opportunity to doubt his skills because of his shortcomings.

As Callan reached for his phone, footsteps thundered towards his office. Robert clutched the doorframe, panting, 'There's been a call from Hailey Noah. She's reported a break-in.'

It was a stormy night. Dry leaves swirled with the wind, and the overcast sky had now shattered into rain.

Callan drove his unmarked police vehicle, muttering curses at the poor heating in the car. How had this scorching day dwindled into such a terrible night?

He raced as fast as he could, but the bloody car wouldn't let him drive full throttle.

Eventually, he arrived at Abigail's Arty World. It was a quiet neighbourhood with meagre streetlights. The quaint yards lay deserted, and the lights in most houses were off. The residents would be tucked up in their beds. The urge to get out of the sickening rain into warmth tugged at him, yet duty called.

He parked beside the artist's shop.

The flat and the shop were dark too. There was no vehicle in the driveway or any other sign of life.

Where was Hailey?

Drawing his gun out of the holster, Callan, with as little noise as possible, blended into the shadows. The gravel crunched under his feet, thrashing rain dwarfed the sound. Long shadows paired with the still silence and dark house made it feel like he was walking through a graveyard.

Hell, they didn't call this the graveyard shift for nothing!

As he neared the front door of the other half of the cottage, it creaked open and a feeble silhouette stood, shadowed by the awning.

Hailey could've been a ghost, but he didn't believe in the supernatural.

The frail woman stepped outside, hunched against the wind. She gestured for him to enter.

Callan made a dash for the front door, eager to get out of the downpour.

Hailey hugged her arms around her midsection. The flimsy shirt she wore didn't stave off the chill night – she shivered, rocking from side to side. Was it from the cold or terror?

The streetlights cast long shadows inside the dark house. They made Hailey resemble a sunken skeleton, with delicate bones and a pale disposition.

Hadn't Callan described her mother just so a few hours ago?

The door clicked shut behind him, and Callan blinked to adjust to the pitch darkness inside. He slid his gun in place and stared into blackness.

'Where are the lights?' he said in a hushed tone, reaching for his torch.

Hailey trembled as she stuttered. 'I-I didn't know what to do. I swear I heard a noise in the store.'

The white beam of his torch struck the pale pink walls and illuminated a bare corridor. 'When did ye hear this noise?'

Hailey flinched, the white glow from the torch making

her appear scared and sickly. 'I called the station right away. Switched the lights off and hid in the storage cabinet.'

That was fifteen minutes ago.

Her voice was so soft, Callan had to lean in to hear. 'Did ye check the store out?'

Hailey bit her lip like she was trying to keep her teeth from chattering. 'No, I-I'm sorry. I didn't want to let them know I was here.'

Callan narrowed his eyes. 'Of course. Could it have been yer mother or the wind?'

Hailey placed a hand on the pink walls, as if bracing herself. 'Mama always has the van with her. I'd have heard it. I peeped out of my window too, after everything was silent for a while, just – just before ye came. The back door to the shop's open.'

'Alright. Please stay in here. Ye can put a light on if ye want. Are the doors and windows in here locked? Or should I check out this place first and then the store?'

Hailey's eyes widened. 'No, there's not been any sound in here, and everything's locked. I locked up like I always do before sundown. I'm sure about it. Please, please check the store out.'

He hadn't pegged Hailey as a scaredy-cat.

Nodding, Callan headed for her front door. Hailey whispered, 'Callan? I think ye should try the back door to the shop. I heard the sound there – it was in the back.'

Hailey's side of the house didn't have a back door, so Callan had to tiptoe around the building to make his way towards the backyard.

He'd pulled his gloves on so he didn't contaminate the scene.

There was a tiny patch of green lawn cordoned off by a hedge. Unlike Cosimo and Jason, Hailey looked after this garden. The hedges too grew in a disciplined manner.

Callan clung to the stone facade of the building. A stray bit of ivy scratched his face, and the rough stone scraped against his calloused palm.

He pushed the ivy away and surveyed the backyard. Hailey was right: the back door of the store was wide open, lightly creaking and groaning in the breeze.

The rain's vengeance had died to a patter, although the previous downpour had Callan soaked from head to toe. Damn it!

He didn't have a spare set of clothes either, thanks to his car being towed away.

Whoever it was that had broken in was probably long gone. Or had fled once they'd heard his car approach. But Callan would take no chances.

Somewhere in the trees an owl hooted, sending fissures through the silence.

From under his coat pocket, Callan pulled out his gun again and inched towards the back entrance.

Who could it have been? What would someone want at an artist's shop? Gold? Silver?

He ducked by the doorway, back against the wall and gun at the ready. The wind sent the hedges and trees rustling, and the open door swayed.

Holding his breath, he kicked the door so that it opened fully and flashed his torch inside.

Darkness stared back. The air held its breath.

The two work tables had various tools and equipment placed haphazardly. A block of wood perched on one work desk like a stout pigeon. The other work desk was cleaner. Hailey had shut the drawers tight. A few larger tools were hooked onto the walls, placed in a line. Nothing was out of place.

Nothing except the ajar door.

Callan cocked his head and surveyed the room with his torch. His boots snapped against the stone floor as he inspected the workshop and the store beyond.

Amongst the many trinkets and ornaments lining the shelves, nothing looked broken or missing. Some dust had settled on a couple of shelves from the woodwork the artists were carrying out in the studio.

No visible damages.

The glass door that led into the shop was shut, the glass still intact.

A certain stillness hung in this dusty room. It was as if all the tiny statues and doll houses were standing still, watching him. A few dreamcatchers hung from the ceiling. They were statues, their feathers not fluttering even a wee bit.

The only sounds were his treads on the floor, coupled with his own breaths. He placed his gun in its holster and smoothed his coat. There was no one here.

For the last time, he perused the workshop and inspected the alarm. Aye, someone had disengaged it – if it had been on in the first place.

There were no signs of cut wires, so if it had been disengaged, whoever it was must have had the keys. Apart from Adelaide and Hailey, who had keys to the shop?

If it was a thief, what were they looking for?

With one last swivel of his torch, Callan stopped short at the computer in the shop's corner. The till. Of course – thieves were cash hungry.

Hailey had switched off the computer, but a glint under it caught his eye. He felt around, fingers curling around a handle. It was a drawer to store cash. Callan tugged at it, yet it didn't give. The small desk also had a card machine, now switched off.

Bending lower, Callan inspected the floor and found splotches of mud. Ah, so someone had been here in this damp weather. It had been pouring off and on for a couple of hours, though. What's to say it wasn't from earlier when Hailey or her mother billed a customer?

Someone had to have walked through mud though – used the yard instead of the driveway.

Callan hooked a finger into another tiny drawer of the desk and tugged it out.

It revealed heaps of paper. Bloody hell! The situation in his office had got so bad, paper now terrified him. Brilliant!

Having rubbed shoulders with Aileen, he figured these were invoices. So he read through the details, his torch highlighting the date. They were the most recent.

If what Aileen would've said was right, these were invoices waiting for an accountant to log them in… But what would a thief do with an invoice?

He left that thought churning in his mind before stepping out and shutting the door behind him.

Callan inspected the bushes right behind the store, but came up empty-handed. There was nothing – no footprints in the mud or any sign someone had trampled the grass.

The hedges weren't too high on either side of the house and the stone wall was about waist high, hardly a deterrent for a thief.

He flashed the torch around, yet all it illuminated were the eerie eyes of a bat.

He heard it screeching, and the back window to Hailey's flat opened. She trembled, clutching the frame tightly. 'Did ye –did ye find anything?'

'Give me a minute.'

She shut the window and disappeared.

He flashed the torch in the side bushes. There! A size-seven shoe it looked like.

So someone *was* here.

Callan switched off his torch and knocked on Hailey's front door. The door opened at once, and she ushered him in.

Hailey had switched on the lamp in the living room.

It was a sparsely decorated area, especially for an artist.

A sofa faced the small TV, and a desk sat by the window overlooking the driveway. There was a picture hanging on the wall, a photograph of the loch.

It was strange for an artist to have such bare walls. If he remembered right, her mother painted pieces of modern art. So who had snapped this photograph? Hailey herself?

There were no pictures of family, pets, or friends. Was Hailey a loner?

She sank into the chair by the desk, arms still around herself and eyes too wide on her pale face.

She'd tied her hair back, yet a few strands escaped. She slouched as if scared to sit to her full height.

Callan stood awkwardly to the side, dripping water onto the floor, yet Hailey didn't object. 'There's no one there. Are ye sure ye didn't leave the door open in yer haste?'

Hailey's voice was soft, barely a whisper. 'I always lock the place when I leave. It's a habit. My Mama, she insists on it. We're working on a lot of different pieces at the moment, and we can't afford a theft.'

'Are ye certain ye locked the door?'

'Aye, I am. I always double-check.'

'And did ye reactivate the alarm?'

She halted for a split second, her mouth forming an O.

'Aye, I believe I did.' Her conviction wavered with every answer.

Callan scrawled it all in his notepad, trying not to let the water droplets splotch the ink. 'Did ye lock the place alone? Was yer mother with ye?'

Hailey shook her head. 'I was alone. Mama went home early. She wasn't feeling well.'

The sound of Callan's pen scratching the paper was loud in the room. He'd seen Adelaide a few hours ago. Unwell? It couldn't be further from the truth, not unless something drastic had happened. Fayola and Adelaide had to have exchanged words again. Their thundering rows were infamous in town.

Whoever had taken the invoice, it wasn't Adelaide – it couldn't be. Why would she jump over the wall and leave without locking up?

Callan frowned as he stared out the window. There were no overt signs of a break-in, so the most likely option was that whoever it was had possessed a key.

Hailey knuckled her eyes. 'Sorry, it's been the strangest week.'

'Why do ye call it strange?'

The dim lamp tickled Hailey's pale skin, making it glow yellow. She bit her lips and contemplated what to say. 'For starters, ye reopened Blaine's case. Then this break-in. And… And Mama said ye questioned her about a pendant?'

So Adelaide had informed Hailey about it. Whether by asking her to look through the order books or in a rage, Callan couldn't tell. 'Do ye ken anything about a bird-shaped pendant?'

Hailey shook her head far too quickly. She was distraught – her shoulders shivered and her breaths were shallow.

'What do ye keep in the drawer by the till? Apart from receipts, I mean.' Callan's pen hovered over his notepad.

She turned to him, eyebrows furrowed. 'The pending or recently paid receipts our accountant hasn't filed away yet.'

'Have ye had any customers who wanted to keep their dealings secretive?'

For the first time, Hailey smiled. It was a genuine, open smile. 'Plenty! Name any young man who wants a customised promise ring or engagement ring done. We haven't got a jeweller in town, so this is the place they come. We make pieces using precious metals and outsource the engagement rings to a vendor in the next town.'

Hell, this was useless. Why would a man asking a woman to marry him steal an invoice?

His sister had taken great joy in torturing him with a reality show about 'bridezillas', but even that crazy lot never went as far as to steal an invoice.

Callan cleared his throat. He had to get back to the station and get dry. He addressed Hailey in a gentler tone despite the anger burbling inside him. 'Could ye have a look around the shop now?'

Eyes wide, she shook her head.

'Why don't I come back in the morning after ye've had time to go through the workshop?'

Hailey's shoulders sagged as if she'd been braced for an attack. Her breath stuttered and her eyes misted.

Callan's work here was done. He couldn't help, especially since nothing appeared out of place. Hailey would have to report what had gone missing – if anything.

First Candace Willoughby and now Hailey Noah, two people connected to Blaine.

Callan hated coincidences.

If someone had broken into the shop, this had to do with the missing person case.

He needed to inform Rory about this.

For now, only the morning would bring some answers.

CHAPTER EIGHT

Aileen's incessant pacing could've plucked the hairs off the carpet. She didn't notice the soft fur tickling her bare feet or the calming scent of dried lavender hanging by the window. Her thoughts preoccupied her.

The day had been a strange one. She'd got so used to Callan: solving cases together, bickering and joking with one another.

Her loud sigh echoed in the room. Outside the locked windows, rain pelted against the glass. Earlier this summer, a similar setting of thunder and rain had given her the most heinous shock: a dangling corpse. Aileen sighed again. She didn't want to think about it.

Her mind hopped back to the happenings of recent days.

After an invigorating self-defence session with Callan, she'd asked him to dinner. He hadn't responded. Then, according to Isla, he'd been slogging away on this case of his missing friend. And the next thing she knew, he'd allegedly assaulted an old woman, his friend's piano teacher.

What was going on with Callan? Why had he built up walls?

A loud voice poked through her thoughts. *He's bored with you.*

Aileen paused mid-stride. Had her constant nagging or her urge to be orderly bored him? They had no interests in common, especially since she didn't keep abreast with the latest of the latest.

But Callan didn't keep up with trends either. Heck, he couldn't tell one social media app from the other, unless it pertained to a case.

Aileen's feet took to pacing again.

Had he reconnected with Patricia?

A loud voice jeered, *You don't stand a chance next to a tall blond woman. Patricia is ambitious and brave.*

That made sense. She didn't hold a candle to Patricia. Hell, the couple of times she'd seen her strutting down the street, people had stopped in their tracks to gape at her.

Aileen tossed her unremarkable brown locks over her shoulder.

The clock struck midnight, yet Aileen couldn't find even the tiniest sliver of sleep. Tired? Yes, weariness blanketed her, her heart heavy. But sleep? There weren't any tendrils of sleep in her eyes.

The phone shrilled, startling her. She jogged towards where it charged by her bed and unplugged it, knocking a book to the floor. 'Hello?'

A loud voice boomed through the line. 'How's ma murder-magnet grandwean?'

All the pent-up tension in her muscles evaporated in the blink of an eye.

'Do you know what time it is?' She tried to sound exasperated, but a grin spoiled it.

'Why's a hale and hearty wean like ye going to bed by twelve? Ye should be up all night, making—'

'Gran!'

Siobhan Mackinnon didn't know the meaning of boundaries, and her boisterous nature often meant she asked any question which came to mind.

She pried all the time, yet Aileen's ears warmed and her blush crept lower to her neck. 'I don't want to hear the end of—'

'Ye're no fun. At your age, Eddie and I didn't give two hoots. Off we went, painting the town red. Hell, *he* worried about *ma* reputation. I told him I'd drowned reputation before I was born. He realised he had to be careful about his virtue.'

A roaring laugh escaped Aileen. Only Siobhan could've said those words. She could picture Eddie Mackinnon, the ex-thief and grandfather she'd never met, worried about himself. Since Siobhan had finally confessed their secret, Aileen had coaxed her gran into telling her more stories about him, each more riotous than the last.

'What's going on with you? Why aren't you glued to the TV with a whisky in hand?'

Siobhan grumbled. 'I refused to eat the sorry excuse of tomato soup they serve here. Nancy's cross with me. She's taken all ma secret stash away and also stolen the remote! All I can see now are meditation videos. I dinnae need to bloody meditate; I need ma whisky.'

Aileen grinned: ninety, naughty and adored. Siobhan never pretended otherwise. She rambled, clearly distressed. 'Ye need to come here and bring yer blue-eyed boyfriend. I think ma room's bugged. No, I ken ma room's bugged. How else would she ken where I keep my whisky?'

Aileen laughed again, unable to hold it in. Siobhan's nurse knew exactly where she kept her hidden treasures: chocolate bars, whisky, and candy. All items her doctor had warned her against.

Siobhan didn't pay any heed to her doctor's instructions; nor did she show any respect for rules.

The word 'boyfriend' echoed in Aileen's mind.

'I don't have a boyfriend, Gran.'

Callan hadn't given her the time of day.

Siobhan let out a string of profanities a grandmother shouldn't have in her repertoire. 'Life's too short to not talk to each other. Bicker but make-up in the next heartbeat. Eddie and I argued all the time. Well, it's the—'

Aileen drowned out the X-rated part that no grandmother should say to her grandchild.

Her gran's high-spirited words lifted her sombre mood, though. 'Callan and I are friends. At least, I thought we were. I don't know why he isn't speaking to me.'

'His loss!' Siobhan said firmly. 'Ye're a catch and I'm not saying so cause ye're ma grandwean. Look at ye: a business owner, coveted forensic accountant and now a serial murder-catcher – like a dreamcatcher. Besides, ye're beautiful. Why, I looked like you at your age, but I had two sons too.'

Aileen grunted. Her gran didn't often pay compliments. Did she do so now to boost her spirits, or did she have an ulterior motive?

'Now, I'd like ye to be bolder with him. He's a shy sort, so if he isn't taking the first step, you should. Reach out to him. If he's hare-brained, ye don't need him, do ye? If he's got a loaf up there, ye can show him what he's missing.'

It sounded like Siobhan had a ready-made plan. When Aileen asked her about it, her gran demanded she get her notepad out. Despite her age, Siobhan had one too many tricks up her sleeve, and she'd given this some serious thought. When the clock struck one, Aileen had an entire blueprint written down, but would she go through with the plan?

❄

RORY HAD A MEETING WITH THE LOCAL COUNCIL ABOUT the incident with Candace Willoughby. When Rory had informed Callan of it, his heart had lodged in his throat.

What would convince them he hadn't hurt the old woman?

The morning dawned sunny, without a hint of the previous night's storm. The air blew with a flavour of the damp mud after the night's rain.

Callan turned into Adelaide's Arty World. He'd brought Officer Robert Davis to study the footprint in the hedges.

Robert carried a small kit with him and asked Callan questions. 'So this footprint could belong to a male or a female?'

Callan jabbed a finger towards the house and got out of the car.

The two burly officers rounded the storefront and made their way towards the hedge.

The bright sunlight should help them study the footprint.

Robert crouched, lips pursed as he studied the ground. A few leaves had fallen, covering the exposed mud.

Pulling on gloves, Robert swatted the leaves away, careful not to disturb the print.

'A size seven. Ye were right about that. And they look like boots.' On hands and knees, he bent lower until his nose touched the soggy earth. 'I guess there's a logo on it, but I can't make it out. Hold on.' He reached into his bag.

Callan crossed his arms and watched Robert take pictures of the print. Holding the camera under their noses, the officers studied the faint markings of a logo.

'Do ye recognise it?' Callan didn't have a head for fashion. He couldn't tell one brand from the other.

The police constable could. He whistled when the lens zoomed in. 'It's a fancy one, it is. My wife wants one of these. She's building a kitty for herself, in an actual piggy bank. The picture of a shoe from this brand looms over our bed, something to do with manifesting.'

'Print these out and see what Rory says about them.'

Busy snapping more pictures, Robert grunted.

'I'll go meet with Hailey and Adelaide. See what's been taken.' He marched towards the shop, leaves, grass, and gravel crumbling under his feet.

The ivy that had scratched him in last night's darkness bloomed verdant, clutching the stone walls like a bairn to his mother.

The door to the store tinkled open as he stepped inside, only to be hit with the aroma of rosemary. What happened to the roses he'd smelled last time? He eyed the quirky chime shimmering like ocean waves.

Careful not to break anything on any of the shelves, Callan made his way to the back. When everything had been still last night, causing goosebumps to prick his skin, now light bathed it in cheeriness.

He noticed a few statues and ornaments he'd missed in the darkness. They were pretty.

Callan knocked on the wooden door that led to the workshop in the back. They hadn't shut it last night. They just used it as a barrier during the day between the workshop and the store...

But what if a customer walked in and stole a piece? Would Adelaide notice them? So much for being unable to afford a theft.

It took a while for someone to answer his knock. Adelaide stood in the doorway, frowning. 'What?'

Callan clenched his jaw. 'Yer daughter reported a break-in last night. I'd asked her to go through the shop and check what they stole.'

Adelaide crossed her arms and gave him a once-over. 'Detective, please step in.'

She made way for him.

Wooden slabs, nails, screws and a chisel littered the two work desks.

Hailey hunched over one desktop, working on a tiny artefact so minute she used a magnifying glass. She didn't look up; nor did she greet him, continuing her work as if he didn't exist.

Adelaide motioned for Callan to take a seat at the other workplace. He shook his head and gestured for Adelaide to sit instead.

Her frail shoulders slouched, wrinkles crumpling her forehead. A large silver ring glistened on her bony hand. She wore her hair piled up on her head, exposing the wrinkles on her cheeks and forehead. Like her daughter, her skin looked peaky.

'There's been a misunderstanding, Detective.'

Callan raised an eyebrow. 'Misunderstanding?'

Adelaide rolled her eyes to cast a glance at Hailey. 'Aye, Hailey misunderstood. There's been no break-in. She must've left the door open – a human error.'

Out the corner of his eye, Callan saw Hailey flinch.

Interesting.

He asked again, 'Are ye certain nothing's amiss?'

She bobbed her head. 'Absolutely. Nothing's out of place. Everything's as I left it last night.'

Callan observed the room, noticing all the tools were as they had been. 'Do ye always leave before Hailey does?'

She played with a tool on her desk, the veins and bones protruding from the back of her hands. 'If I have work, for example, deliveries to make, I leave early. It depends on my workload. The doctor's asked me to take things slow.'

Poising to take notes, Callan asked, 'Did ye look into the inventory, or whatever ledger ye've got to check the commissions for a chain?'

Adelaide huffed. Her scowl indicated she didn't want to see him, but he had no time for her moods.

'Aye, I did.' She waved her hands dismissively. 'And there is one commission for a silver pendant in the past year. Yer boss commissioned a necklace for his wife. I haven't made a piece with a silver bird on it, ever.'

Silver bird? Callan had never specified the colour of the bird.

Interesting indeed.

The glass chime on the front door tinkled, signalling a new customer. Adelaide straightened. 'I must go see who it is. Please, Detective.'

She gestured for him to walk back into the store ahead of her.

Kicking me out, eh?

Callan tilted his head towards Hailey. 'I would like to have a word with Miss Noah before I leave.'

Adelaide's gaze fluttered between Hailey and him.

'I don't see why. I've answered all yer questions, haven't I?'

Callan kept his tone as polite as he could. 'It's regarding the investigation into Blaine Macgregor.'

Adelaide reluctantly sauntered out towards her customer.

Callan waited to hear her greet them. Then, taking Adelaide's position in the chair, he crossed his arms and gazed at Hailey.

She still didn't look up from her work. He had to get this done before the customer left and Adelaide returned.

'Miss Noah?'

She responded with a grunt.

'Is there anything ye'd like to add to what yer mother said?'

'No,' came the inaudible whisper.

'I hope ye understand not declaring facts to the police is a crime.'

Hailey's hands halted, her tools clattering on the table. Slowly, she turned to him and met his gaze.

He'd seen the fear on her face last night. Now she beheld a sorrowful acceptance. Instead of urging her on, Callan sat still.

With a side glance at the door, Hailey made sure Adelaide bustled behind the customer.

She whispered, spitting out the words in a flurry, 'I-I swear I shut the door last night. As I said, I double-check. Always. There is no way I left the door open. Someone could have opened it. It's a ritual, locking this place.'

Callan raised an eyebrow. 'Is there any way someone can enter the store from yer cottage?'

Hailey's eyes widened. 'No! No, there's no such connecting door. We have separate attics too.'

He'd never heard of such an arrangement before. 'And why is that? Isn't this entire cottage yer own?'

'My mothers'. They initially had a plan to lease the other side of the cottage. Although they ended up using it as well. Now I live there.'

Callen scribbled his notes.

The tapping of Hailey's feet on the floor echoed through the room. She twiddled her thumbs. 'Look, sorry she's being this standoffish. They argued last night – again.'

Adelaide waved at the customer, her jovial laugh carrying over to the workshop.

His timer sounded the gong. Callan lowered his voice. 'Is an invoice missing?'

Hailey frowned, shaking her head. 'I don't—'

A drawer snapped closed outside. She jerked, swivelling back to her work desk. 'If we're done, I've got to get back to work.'

Knowing she'd dismissed him, Callan walked into the shop again and saw a customer exit the shop.

Adelaide's gaze flittered to him.

'I hope ye got what ye were looking for. As ye can see, nothing's amiss. Hailey made a mistake.'

Callan thanked her, walking out the door. He *had* noticed something amiss here. He needed to know what they were arguing about last night. And he had to get a hold of Fayola because this involved her somehow. He *knew* it.

❄

AILEEN PULLED UP IN FRONT OF THE BAKERY.

She'd tossed and turned last night, wondering what had happened to Patricia. The nagging voice questioning if she'd contacted Callan didn't help. Had he helped her out in an unofficial capacity?

Patricia had begged them not to call the police, hadn't she?

Isla gestured from behind the counter. No hugs today –

judging by the look on her friend's face, it had been a long night.

Aileen slid into the window seat, hot chocolate in hand, and stared out.

The buzz of activity and people chattering livened her spirits. The sun blazed, drying the wet roads. A combination of after-rain calm coupled with the sunlight equalled the cosiest weather. Aileen loved it.

The chair next to her scraped against the floor, and Isla plopped into it. 'Ugh, it's been one of those days!'

Aileen playfully rolled her eyes but stopped, her smirk disappearing into a frown when she caught a movement on the opposite footpath. 'What's happening there?'

'Where?' Isla followed her gaze.

On the opposite side of the road, a compact car pulled up. Aileen had seen this car once before. Where?

The windows were tinted, so she couldn't see the driver. But hardly anyone owned such a compact car in Loch Fuar. Most people preferred service trucks and SUVs for the rough terrain. This sort of car wouldn't last on the Highland roads.

The driver's window slid open an inch and a mop of white hair peeked from behind the tinted glass. A jacket-clad hand adjusted the side mirrors, then the windows slid shut, and the driver inched the car ahead.

After a minute, the door opened, and a man uncurled from his seat. He struggled to get his bearings, almost tripping over to face-plant.

Aileen gasped when the sun highlighted his face. 'Isla, it's Mr Edgar!'

Isla licked her lips, enraptured. 'What's he doing here?'

Aileen didn't know, but she wanted to find out.

Edgar rounded the car and pulled something out of his pocket. Without missing a beat, he ducked his head and peered to his right and left before striding away in the opposite direction.

Aileen stood as if to follow him when he disappeared inside a small cottage. 'Where is he going?'

Isla frowned. 'Fayola's old office.'

They waited, hoping their hearts wouldn't beat so loud. Time ticked by slowly.

'Can't we knock on the door?'

Aileen narrowed her eyes at Isla. 'What would you say this time? You want to buy the place?'

She got an eye roll.

An hour later, he still hadn't left.

Isla pushed off the table. 'We need to get to Patricia's. Maybe this is just a hoax.'

Just then, Aileen's phone pinged with a message from an unknown number.

'Shall I compare thee to a summer's day?

Thou art more lovely and more temperate.'

What the—?

Who quoted Shakespeare?

At her baffled expression, Isla peered at her phone and read the quote. 'Who sent you a couplet?'

Aileen shrugged.

'I didn't know you were into poetry, especially stuff by the Bard.'

Aileen shook her head. She hated poetry. It gave her nightmares, and Shakespeare? Panic attacks. It might've been her school teacher's fault more than the great Bard's, but she still didn't read it.

She frowned. 'Just because I know them doesn't mean I like them. Who would send me this?'

Isla mimed a gruff voice. 'Ask and thou shall find out. Hey, maybe it's Callan who's writing to you incognito!'

Isla read too many romance novels. Callan with a poetry book? Aileen could somersault for the Queen.

She typed out a message. *'Who is this?'*

The answer came immediately. *'Sorry, I thought you'd saved my number. This is Gerald.'*

Gerald?

Isla squeaked. 'Och, Aileen, you've got an admirer in Dr Erwin.'

Gerald Erwin had messaged her Shakespearean poetry?

Aileen's stomach flipped. Had she charmed him?

CHAPTER NINE

Callan gripped the steering wheel until his knuckles turned white.

Adelaide wouldn't cooperate. Fayola had disappeared under an indivisibility cloak, and Candace Willoughby was registering a complaint against him.

Someone wanted to keep Blaine's whereabouts a secret, and they were going to extreme lengths to make sure of it.

Assaulting an old woman, pushing the blame on him and now breaking in to Hailey Noah's house.

What important information could an invoice have?

Callan turned right into the police station's lane.

Once inside the coffee-laden office, Callan pointed at Robert. 'Do ye ken Fayola Noah's phone number or a way we can reach her?'

The officer shook his head. 'She's retired. At least my maw thinks so. Best place to get her would be at home, I reckon.'

Callan raced out the door before the air-conditioning could work its magic on his overheated body.

The door to the station clanked shut, only to be thrown open a moment later. 'Wait up!'

Robert jumped into the car as Callan took off.

❄

The houses in this area were larger and the driveways longer. Professional gardeners tended to most of the manicured lawns. Cigarette stubs didn't litter the roads, and exotic aromas scented the air.

Fayola Noah had done well for herself in business, and her house stood as a testament to her stellar career.

It gleamed modern-white, as if someone had repainted it recently. The long driveway sat empty, and to Callan's dismay, the grilled gate was locked.

He parked the car by the kerb and strolled towards the intercom. He buzzed the bell and waited, tapping his foot on the cobbled pavement.

Robert fidgeted, shuffling his legs and peeking at the neighbourhood. 'Why are we here?'

When they got no answer, Callan muttered a curse. 'Adelaide and Fayola had one of their rows last night. Think, Robert, if someone broke into yer wife's salon, would ye be by her side when the police came questioning or go about yer business as if nothing's gone wrong?'

The green officer contemplated the situation. 'Aye, even if we argued, I'd be there for her. I never wondered why Mrs Noah didn't stick around.'

And apparently, she didn't answer the bell either. A sliver of trepidation bloomed in Callan's gut. He considered hopping over the fence, but in view of the complaint being registered against him, he thought better of it.

Instead, he pressed the buzzer again, as if it would magically open the damn gate.

Two minutes passed, and she still hadn't answered.

Bloody hell!

A man rounded the corner wearing grey shorts and a florescent yellow sweatshirt. He panted as he jogged at a steady pace.

Seeing the two of them, especially the uniformed Robert, he came to a halt by the gate. 'Can I help ye?'

Callan pointed at the house. 'We're looking for Mrs Fayola Noah.'

Using a wristband, he swiped the sweat off his forehead. 'Hard luck finding her – she's off on a yoga retreat. They must've had another go at it. Fayola usually leaves after a nasty fight.'

What could they have been arguing about last night?

Callan nodded at the man. 'Thank ye, Mr…'

The man chuckled. 'Ye don't recognise me, do ye? Rory's my paw. Ye must be Callan and Robert. Paw's sure proud of the two of ye.' He waved. 'I've got to get back before my lunch break's over.'

Callan stared after Rory's son.

All these years and Callan had never met Rory's family. Rory had invited him to his house, but Callan always declined, and eventually Rory had stopped asking.

For Callan, work equalled work, and he didn't want to intermingle it with his personal life.

He ran a hand through his sweat-covered scalp. Hell, before Aileen, he hadn't had a private life at all. And now, all those years he'd dedicated to police work were under question. All because some eejit thought it cool to wear black and assault an old woman in his name.

He growled, nails digging into his palm.

Callan would find him and make the sod pay.

❄

A COUPLE OF MINUTES AFTER THREE IN THE AFTERNOON, Aileen and Isla set out for Patricia's house again.

Carly had bawled her eyes out at lunchtime, leaving Daniel harried. The burly man could wrestle with a polar bear, but his bairn's tears brought him to his knees.

Aileen, driving this time, left Isla with a lot of energy to chat. 'I think it's an excellent idea. If this person, by some miracle, hadn't seen us, changing cars would be cool. I wish we could be Bond.' She held aloft two fingers and in a gruff voice said, 'James Bond.'

Isla laughed at her own joke, making Aileen giggle at her antics. 'Looks like someone had a good night despite the tantrum.'

Isla sighed exaggeratedly. 'Carly fussed through the night, which meant I barely got my eight hours. But well, once you have a bairn with a husband who's scared of tears, you get used to it.'

Carly could sleep through storms, but her new teeth kept her up. She was a handful – a sweet handful.

Shifting in her seat to face Aileen, Isla furrowed her eyebrows. 'What about Mr Edgar?'

Aileen huffed. 'I didn't expect to see him at Fayola's old office. He's kept himself inside his room ever since we went to Blaine's house. He came down for breakfast but just went straight back to his room after. Oh, he asked me if we had room service at Dachaigh. I had some leftovers, and he said he would heat those up and eat. To be honest, he appeared forlorn.'

'And Fayola, do you have any news about her? Did she drop by Dachaigh or contact you?'

'No, she didn't. Mr Edgar said nothing about it either. I reckon she hadn't told him. I think they're friends.'

'What business did he have in her office, Aileen?'

'If I knew, we wouldn't be doing this!'

Aileen turned into the lane leading to Gerald Erwin's clinic. Patricia's shop sat in one of the smaller adjacent alleys.

'I think I'll park the car here, so whoever notices us won't assume we're at Patricia's. A little precaution can go a long way.' Aileen studied the sunshine. 'Hope it doesn't rain.'

Isla hopped out of the car. 'Don't jinx it.'

A few puddles from last night remained scattered on the pavement. Aileen carefully avoided those lest her trousers get muddy. She hated sludge and damp shoes.

This time artificial light lit Patricia's shop. They could hear some tinkering through the open windows.

When they hurried inside, Patricia jumped and laid a hand over her heart. 'You scared the hell out of me. Couldn't you call?'

She wore long sleeves and thick make-up, which didn't quite hide her bruises. As if noticing Aileen's stare, she tugged down the left-hand sleeve. Her grey eyes narrowed. 'What do you want?'

Isla ventured towards her desk, but Patricia raised her hand to stop her. 'I told you, leave me be. Don't tell anyone. It's… It's a personal matter. Stay out of it.'

Isla had never been one to back down. 'We just want to talk. You don't have to tell us anything. We can help you clean the mess upstairs. You can't call Daniel to fix all this, can you? He'll ask what happened.'

Tossing her blond hair behind her shoulders, Patricia crossed her arms. The sleeves tugged up to reveal a white bandage round her wrist.

The air smelled of burned metal, which made it too stuffy to be comfortable. Aileen spied a sleeping bag peeking out from behind the wooden counter. She'd spent the night here, had she?

Patricia pursed her lips. 'I don't mind some help with cleaning this mess and such but,' – she held up a finger, – 'no nosing about and not a word of this to a soul. Please.'

They both agreed, wanting to get into the flat upstairs. There must be something they'd missed in the dark. It had been terrifying and confusing, sneaking in.

It couldn't be a coincidence that a man argued with Patricia and destroyed her home just a few days after the police reopened the missing person case.

Thankfully, they didn't need to brave the narrow metal staircase. Patricia had an indoor staircase leading to her living room through a trapdoor.

'It's so cool.' Aileen had to compliment the design. Trapdoors? Such fun!

The rest of the living space? Not so much.

The darkness of last night had hidden some corners in shadow, but now they could see even more toppled furniture, shattered ornaments, and torn cushions.

Hugging herself, Patricia eyed the damage. 'I left after you did and spent the night downstairs. It's the first time I've had the courage to come see the actual damage for myself.'

Isla walked up to Patricia and pulled her close. 'We're here to help. Let's get to work.'

❄

BACK AT THE POLICE STATION, CALLAN STARED AT HIS board. To hell with Rory's orders! If he went down for a crime he didn't commit, how did it matter if he disobeyed his boss?

He'd updated the board, adding all the bits and bobs

he knew so far. Like the previous case he'd solved unofficially, he could solve this one as well.

Albeit he'd had Aileen's tech genius to help last time.

Callan licked his lips, which still had a layer of his late morning coffee. Aileen – he'd think about her later.

His stomach growled, and he realised he'd forgotten to have lunch. He'd buy himself something soon, but first he needed to think.

Blaine had disappeared fifteen years ago on a Sunday. The last people to see him were Patricia and Cosimo.

Gerald said he'd last seen him in school when Blaine bailed on their camping trip.

Callan pointed at Jason's image on the board. He'd worked weekends so he wouldn't have gone on a trip with them.

It was summer, wasn't it? Why would a teen work weekends when he had weekdays free to work?

He scrawled a note in the margins, his gaze moving on to Candace.

What did she mean when she said Blaine had a row with Daniel? What would they fight about, especially regarding him?

Her story didn't fit right.

Callan plopped into his chair and shut his eyes.

What had she said?

'The day he came to me, he sported a bruised lip. It hadn't been his father who split it. He'd had a fight with one of those burly friends of yers. He's a handyman now, as far as I recall.'

Daniel had his shop, but he also did odd jobs.

He needed to speak with him about this.

Callan stood to go chat with the one friend who'd stuck by him through all the curveballs in his life.

How could he ask Daniel such a question?

If someone heard them, Daniel would be the talk of

town, for the wrong reasons. Could Callan accuse his best friend?

He wouldn't do that. Never. Instead, he'd follow up on the other leads first.

Callan sank back into his chair when Robert strolled in.

He waved a letter under Callan's nose. 'This came for ye.'

Callan plucked it out of his hands, his limbs aching under stress. Had it come from the PSD? Had Candace already lodged her complaint?

His hands went cold and clammy.

Throat dry, he tried to steady the blood rushing into his head.

He turned the envelope around and frowned. There wasn't an official logo or return address – there was just the station's address and Callan's name printed on the envelope.

His gut blared an alarm, so he pulled on a pair of gloves.

Robert handed him a paper knife.

Licking his lips, Callan nudged the envelope open and out fell a printed piece of paper.

The plain A4 white sheet held two sentences:

'They think they know, but the truth is death.

Let's see reality at four. See you at the electrician's.'

'Callan, what is it? Ye've paled.' Robert rushed to his side and perused the letter.

'What does it mean?'

'Murder. There's about to be a murder.' Callan whispered the words, stuck in a trance.

His stomach growled once more, snapping him out of his daze. The bitter taste stuck to his tongue.

Hell! He couldn't sit on his arse and do nothing. He read the words again.

This lunatic had escalated. He or she had announced a murder intention to a police inspector!

Callan barrelled out of his office when the front door opened and Rory stepped in. He raised both eyebrows at Callan. 'Where are ye going?'

Behind him, Robert spluttered, 'Murder. There's about to be a murder.'

Rory snapped the piece of paper from Callan's hand. 'Electrician's. Ye think Patricia's life is in danger?'

Callan gritted his teeth. The clock struck 3.45 p.m. Enough time to stop the ruffian. 'Permission to head out, sir.'

His boss ran a hand through his hair. 'Go. Here, take the cruiser. Robert! Run this for prints. Let's go!'

Callan sped to Patricia's. What would this crazy person do? Why involve Patricia in this?

Was it some crazy plan to hurt women or everyone who'd last seen Blaine?

❄

THEY SWEPT THE LIVING ROOM FIRST, PICKING THEIR WAY through the debris. Patricia dusted the floor to remove all the cracked glass and bits of ceramic while Isla and Aileen righted the furniture. They didn't speak. The sole sounds were the scraping of wood against the carpeted floor or the chink of glass.

Patricia had a liking for scented candles, which were all now scattered on the floor. Asking her permission, Isla lit a soothing lavender one. 'It helps calm the mind.'

With the three of them at it, they got a lot done in record time.

Isla halted her efforts at scrubbing a stubborn stain. 'Should we tackle the kitchen next?'

They dusted and cleaned the kitchen in no time. Aileen opened the windows to let the stench out. The day's heat hadn't helped the bin's odour.

Patricia didn't cook. She had essentials in her larder, and a tiny refrigerator with milk which had curdled. Aileen couldn't help but notice the single knife missing from the knife stand.

It had to be the one the vandal had used to slit the mattress.

Finally, they headed for the bedroom. And from what Aileen recalled, it had been the messiest room of all.

Patricia had shut the door as if it would keep the memories hidden. When she didn't step in to open it, Aileen took matters into her own hands. Despite her show of strength, last night's episode had shaken Patricia. As it would anyone.

Aileen reached for the doorknob just as the doorbell sounded.

Eyebrows scrunched, they all shared a look. Who could it be?

The bell sounded again – twice, four times. Who'd be so frantic to get to Patricia?

Aileen strode over to the front door, since Patricia stood transfixed in the hall.

Now, the person had resorted to pounding on the door like the hounds of hell were nipping at their feet. A gruff voice shouted, 'Patricia! Patricia! Open the bloody door.'

Aileen's step faltered. She'd been so right. In his desperation to meet Patricia, Callan readily banged her door down. But he hadn't the courtesy to respond to Aileen's messages.

Prick!

A cacophony of voices screamed in her head; a hollowness tugged at her heart.

Anger roiling in her gut, Aileen pulled open the door, ready to spit curses when Callan bustled in, knocking her to the floor.

Then his firm arms came around her, holding her to his heaving chest.

Alarm registered in his eyes. 'Aileen?' Then came the anger. 'What the hell are ye doing here? I've had enough of ye putting yerself in danger, woman!'

Aileen tilted her head. 'Such kind words after essentially behaving as if I don't exist!'

Behind her, someone cleared their throat.

Callan's fiery gaze left hers, and his iron-clad grip on her loosened.

Aileen straightened her shirt. What an oaf! He'd never change.

When his eyes landed on Patricia, he heaved a sigh of relief. 'Ye're here. I… Isla.'

Patricia looked between them. 'You called the police! You promised me you wouldn't!'

Callan's eyebrows furrowed. 'What do ye mean? What's going on here?'

So typical of him to barge into someone's house and question them. 'Why are you here?' Aileen asked.

'To prevent a murder.'

The clock struck four, catching Callan's eye.

He pulled out his gun. 'I need to check yer premises. I got a letter threatening yer life, Patricia.'

A collective gasp echoed through the room. What nonsense was he spouting?

Was Callan ill?

She fisted her hands, tempted to check his temperature. The man had lost his mind.

Aileen focused on the lavender. Thank God for the scented candle.

But it did her little good. After what they'd witnessed last night, Aileen couldn't shake away the terror gripping her. Would someone barge in and murder Patricia?

Her heart raced.

Had the murderer already gained entrance and now lay in wait? Had they been here this entire time?

Her anxiety escalated.

Callan disappeared into the kitchen, inspecting the living room next. Finally, he gestured to the closed door. 'Does it lead to the bedroom?'

Mute, Patricia bobbed her head.

His footsteps sounded muffled on the carpeted floor. Every creak of the floorboards reverberated distinctly in the eerie silence.

Laying a hand on the cool metallic doorknob Aileen had gripped a moment ago, he twisted it.

The door groaned.

Callan took a step in and stopped.

His eyes shut when a rancid stink burned through the lavender. Melancholy gripped Aileen's heart and sent it flipping in the most uncomfortable way.

Isla peeked around Callan. 'What? What is it? Blimey! Fayola?'

Glutton for punishment that she was, Aileen peeked into Patricia's destroyed bedroom, which was now awash in light.

It lit up the scene.

A willowy person was sprawled on Patricia's soiled mattress – Fayola, her braided hair spread over the white linens, lay on her side.

A bird-shaped pendant attached to a silver chain dangled from her neck. It caught the sunlight streaming in through the windows.

The chain nor the pendant shocked Aileen, but Fayola did.

Foam coated her lips. Her chest didn't heave; nor did she open her eyes.

Dead.

Someone had murdered Fayola.

CHAPTER TEN

Callan stood in Patricia's bedroom with a scowl on his face and assessed the new crime scene. Everything lay in a mess, including the mattress.

The closed windows trapped the after-effects of death.

Sun beat through the glass, still high in the sky, making Callan's skin prickle.

Who'd done this? And what was Fayola doing here?

Callan crouched to examine the dark blue carpet. The white canvas on the underside of the blue threads stuck out. Patricia had had it for a long time.

He bent lower, focusing on the bristles. Blobs of mud stuck to it. From a shoe?

Callan tugged at the scrubs he wore, the added layer unwelcome in this boiling room. The bloody things itched uncomfortably but were necessary – he'd never do anything to compromise a crime scene.

Feet covered in shoe covers, he found a couple more muddy crumbs between the door and the bed. They were so tiny, one could easily miss them. He didn't find an impression of a foot, at least not with the naked eye.

He moved over to the window side but spotted no mud there.

Fayola Noah lay on the destroyed mattress; her skin had lost its radiance.

He needed the medical examiner to pronounce life extinct. The foam coating her cracked lips gave him an inkling as to what could be the cause of death. He reined himself in and focused on committing the scene to memory.

She wore a long skirt and suede boots, the heels dangling over the bed. She'd been a tall woman. Had she died here?

Callan scratched his chin. It was hard to tell.

He turned to the soles of her boots.

Ah, explains the mud.

There were a few mud splatters on the black suede at the heel of the foot as well. It had been raining yesterday and there were still a few puddles on the road. So Fayola had been outdoors.

The hem of her skirt had some splatters too, although they were negligible. Puddles – it had to be, or soggy mud. If it were pouring, her clothes would've been damp and her shoes muddier.

Callan rounded the bed to crouch next to Fayola's face. She could've been sleeping, and she was – forever.

After a brief examination, he noted no rashes, spots, marks, or bruises on her skin. Her hair lay tucked in neat braids.

She probably didn't fight back.

Callan sat on his heels. Why? Didn't she have a chance?

If Fayola trusted her killer, they'd probably met up. And if she didn't notice them, they'd acted with haste and precision.

Was she meeting her killer? It would be more sinister if she'd trusted the sod. Callan scrawled his observation on the notepad.

Done with his scrutinisation, he checked the top drawer by the bedside. It had a few of Patricia's belongings: a journal, pen, accessories, and a full bottle of sleeping pills, all scattered around.

Where had the medical examiner got to?

A mess of items lay scattered on the bedside table. Someone had removed the lower drawer and flung it to the floor. Cards, trinkets and a smashed photo frame lay on the carpet, some shards of glass visible under the bed.

The top of the bedside lamp hung at an awkward angle to the base.

Heavy treads led to the door. They revealed the scrub-wearing ME and his boss, Rory.

The medical examiner set to work immediately and pronounced life extinct. Using the plethora of tools in her kit, she examined the body. 'I'll need to work on her to give you details, Detective.'

Vomit gurgled from his stomach at the stench and the heat. Callan left the room as more of the forensic team strode in. Best of luck to them.

He let them pass before descending the iron staircase and paused, studying the unkempt yard.

A whiff of rosemary from Adelaide's shop would do him some good.

Callan ran a hand through his damp hair, then pulled out a black handkerchief to mop the rivulets of sweat blazing down his neck and cheeks.

Blast the bloody summer heat! Why couldn't they have winter all year long?

'Callan.' Rory came to a halt beside him. He jabbed a thumb over his shoulder. 'There's a crowd gathered outside, thanks to the sirens. Robert and some firefighters are keeping the mob at bay.'

They stood, shoulders brushing, staring into space, pregnant with awkward silence. Callan braced for the reprimand. Rory would take him off this case, too.

'I assume the note concerned Fayola, not Patricia.'

Callan hissed. 'It makes no sense why she'd be here.'

'Aileen and Isla too, don't ye think?' Rory jerked his head towards the two fiends. 'Speak with them. This is yours.'

It took a while for Rory's words to register. Callan blinked. 'I thought—'

'I've kent ye since ye were a wee lad. Judging by the poor company ye kept, ye could've done worse, yet here ye are – a detective.' Rory looked Callan dead in the eyes. 'I never doubted ye. It pissed me off to think someone had purposefully framed my detective. I dealt with it by the book.'

Now lost for words, Callan gaped like a fish. What… How… Why had Rory taken him off the case?

Questions flooded his mind, paralysing Callan.

Rory crossed his arms, his eyes still unflinching. 'I'm personally investigating Ms Willoughby's case. In the meantime, I want ye to find the bastard who killed Fayola. I have a feeling it'll lead us to whoever thinks it's okay to frame an officer of the law.'

Callan swallowed, overwhelmed and stricken. His boss trusted him, despite the evidence and the witnesses.

What more could he ask for?

'Th-Thank ye.' He'd be always grateful to this man and indebted. 'I will find this bastard. I give my word, sir.'

Rory bobbed his head and strode away.

Callan used the earthy fragrance of the backyard to

settle his stomach and drown out the noise in his head. His eyes met Aileen's.

'Police station,' he mouthed.

❄

CALLAN SLURPED HIS WARM COFFEE AND STARED AT AILEEN over the rim.

She sat ramrod straight in his chair, meeting his gaze with steely eyes. Neither of them blinked.

Was this a stare-off where the first to blink loses?

Knowing he was behaving childishly, Callan flicked his blues to the paper-strewn desk. Damn papers, they'd bury him!

Aileen cleared her throat, her tone not even close to lukewarm. 'Looks like you cleaned up a bit, hereabouts.'

He had cleared off a chunk, yet the papers had somehow duplicated overnight to cause more mess, almost undoing his previous day's work.

Callan took another sip to swirl the sludge in his cup around. He bought himself some time, but damn if he knew what to say.

His eyes sought Aileen's once more.

She raised an eyebrow. 'Well?'

Being a bastard, he deserved her ire. His mother had instilled manners in him and he hadn't stuck by them. So when by some miracle his sister had found out that he'd ghosted Aileen, she'd ratted him out to his mother.

And last night, he'd had a call where – for a long hour – his mother had burned his ear off. She always forgot he was thirty-three, not three.

'I...' He licked his lips. Sometimes he behaved like a three-year-old. Bloody hell, he sucked at this!

On autopilot, his emotions switched to anger.

'What were ye thinking, working this case? It's dangerous!'

Far too calm, Aileen crossed her legs. The action sent a shiver of trepidation through him. 'If you'd have bothered to answer my messages or calls, we'd have worked this case together.'

How did this woman not understand danger, especially after what she'd gone through a month and a half ago?

Trouble. She personified trouble with a capital T. And he had to protect her for her own good.

A heavy mushrooming silence suspended between them.

Aileen chuckled dryly. 'You call me here and now you don't say a word. I don't understand you, Callan. One moment you make me laugh like a loon and the next you won't answer my calls or messages. I'm leaving.'

Callan thudded the mug down on a stack of paper and plopped into his chair. What should he say to her? A lot had gone through his mind in the short drive from Patricia's to the station.

He fingered the crisp paper.

Aileen sighed when he continued to stare at the table. She didn't make a move to leave, though. It gave him some hope, more time.

'Say it, Callan. It's nothing I haven't heard before. Countless times in fact.'

Eyebrows furrowed, he shook his head. 'I don't—'

Her watery eyes stopped him short. Shit, is this how badly he'd affected her?

Bloody git! He'd have punched himself.

She blinked, not looking him in the eye. 'I'm boring. It's not news. I've been expecting it. You don't want to see me anymore. There, I've said the words for you.'

What? Why was she spouting this nonsense again?

A muscle in his jaw twitched. 'Haven't I told ye already ye're anything but "riskless"?' He motioned haphazardly, indicating where they were. 'Here ye are, after finding another body, telling me ye've been sleuthing on yer own. We're arguing about it, aren't we? Ye're a magnet for trouble, Aileen.'

Aileen's uncertain gaze met his before drifting away again.

'Hell! Aileen.' His heart performed a painful somersault. She riled him up and made him helpless all at the same time.

'Come on, Aileen!' he growled. 'I've been busy. If ye dinnae ken, things aren't going well for me – at all.'

'I know.' Her voice sounded timid. 'You're a good person. And… And you aren't alone.'

How could she say such words when all of Loch Fuar was treating him like a criminal?

'Isla believes you can't have hurt the old woman. I-I believe in you too.'

Her words were the balm he'd waited for. They washed over him like cold water over a man burned.

She held such sway over him. Lord, help him now.

Callan slammed his office door shut and crouched in front of Aileen. He didn't want their conversation to end up in tomorrow's gazette. 'I'm sorry for the way I behaved. My judgement got the better of me.'

'You never told me about your relationship with Blaine. I thought we were partners, friends even.'

More than that.

Callan coughed at his heart's insistence. He believed in truth, so he stuck to it. 'I visited Patricia the same morning for questioning and she commented about my leg – or lack thereof.'

The tears in her eyes evaporated in smoke, replaced by

red-hot fire. 'She did *what*? What a prick!' Aileen smacked Callan's shoulder. 'What do you see in her?'

'Poison.' The word came easily.

'Why do you want her back then?'

Back? He never wanted Patricia in his life again. Not like the teenaged eejit he'd been had. He knew what was good for him, and the healthiest antidote sat in front of him.

'When did I ever— What do ye see in the doctor?'

Aileen narrowed her eyes until they were fear-inducing slits. 'Are you stalking me? How do you know about him?'

'I saw ye at Isla's Bakery!' his voice boomed through the silent room.

'And you jumped to conclusions?' She matched his decibel level.

'After what Patricia and he said to me? Of course!'

Aileen shoved him so hard he tumbled on the floor. 'Fool!'

Ignoring his string of profanities, she paced. 'He's up to some mischief.'

Obviously! She'd been besotted with the man!

For the first time since they'd met, Aileen muttered 'bastard' and followed it up with 'bampot'. Scottish profanities, like the rhyme of a bagpipe, poured from her mouth.

Wow…

'I head to Isla's almost every day at around noon, after I'm done with all my chores for the morning. Not once have I seen him there. And now he bumps into me and insists I join him for coffee? He's got my female intuition ringing alarm bells.'

Callan frowned. Aileen's hair flailed all over the place, like she'd been tugging at it. The neat and tidy version of her had disappeared.

He dared only to whisper. 'Yer intuition's telling ye he's interested.'

'I'm not an eejit. I sense right from wrong! And I've dealt with a fair share of crazy men. I can tell there's a part of him that's not genuine.'

So he hadn't been wrong about the smooth-talking bastard. 'What's wrong, do ye think?'

Striding towards where her bag lay, Aileen pulled out her yellow notepad.

For the first time, he grinned without inhibition. Aileen was a picture: hair scattered, a reddish flush on her cheeks and her fiery brown eyes set on her customary yellow notepad.

It happened for the first time in a while. Adrenaline rushed through his body, flooding his veins as it always did when he embarked on an investigation. And now, Aileen's presence in his office, in front of the fresh murder board, her notepad in hand, gave him the rush. It tugged familiar and exciting, an omen of interesting times to come.

And he readied himself to do this. With his partner.

❄

CALLAN RAN A HAND THROUGH HIS HAIR.

Aileen had given him a rundown of everything she'd seen and done regarding the case. And the more she said, the more intermingled the events became.

'Ye've seen Fayola with yer guest at Blaine's old house.'

'Yes, and someone's murdered her now with a chain around her neck. It's the same chain.' Aileen pointed to the image of the chain around Candace's wrist on the board.

It was impossible. How did two chains have his name on them?

Aileen squinted at the board. 'Why is this person targeting you?'

He came up with the only explanation that seemed plausible. 'It's a good technique to divert attention and throw me off the case.'

'You've scared the criminal. They know you'll get to the bottom of this.' Aileen cocked her head. 'And this chain, you said you've spoken to Adelaide about it?'

Callan grunted. 'And Hailey, but when we informed them of Fayola's death, she asked me to come speak with her again. She wants to add to what she told us before.'

❄

THE DOOR OPENED TO REVEAL A STICK-THIN FIGURE: Adelaide.

'Get out!' she barked without a hint of remorse. 'Get out! What are ye good for, anyway? Fayola is dead!'

Stoically, Callan bobbed his head. 'I'm sorry for yer loss. May I send a grievance officer for ye?'

Adelaide gestured wildly. 'I don't need anyone, and I certainly don't want ye loitering about!'

'I do,' came a firm voice from within the dim shadows of the room. Hailey appeared frail, eyes and cheeks red from crying. Her lower lip trembled. She glanced at her mother before speaking in a firm tone. 'If ye would've told him the truth in the first place, this wouldn't have happened.'

Adelaide lunged at her daughter. 'How dare ye!'

Callan pivoted to hold Adelaide back as she spat profanities, gnashing her teeth.

He struggled, Adelaide's fury stronger than her musculature. 'Ma'am, if ye don't stop I will have to call an officer and—'

Adelaide went limp in his arms. 'My own daughter would do this to me?'

Hailey crossed her arms and lifted her chin stubbornly. The first time she'd shown a backbone. 'I'm tired of yer bullying. And this isn't about you.'

Stepping aside, she gestured to Callan and Aileen, who until now had hid behind Callan, watching the show with rapt attention.

Once seated on the sofa in the bare room, Hailey leaned ahead. 'We didn't get any commissions for necklaces shaped like birds.'

Adelaide slumped in the chair at the desk, eyes looking out onto the driveway, yet she was far away.

Callan had his notepad out. He frowned at Hailey.

She stabbed her forefinger in thin air. 'But we did have someone ask us to make their bird-shaped pendant as bright and new as possible.'

Pendant? As in singular? Callan focused on her words.

Hailey spluttered. 'A pendant just like the one I owned as a member of the White Birds group.'

Callan scribbled notes in his illegible hand and waited for Hailey to continue. When she didn't, Aileen pitched in. 'Who asked you to clean the chain?'

Hailey blinked. 'Not only to clean but she also asked us to remove the engraving in the back and add a new one: "Callan".'

'She gave you one chain?'

'Just one.'

'Whose name was on it, Hailey?'

Hailey fiddled with the hem of her shirt. 'Patricia Adair.'

Painful, ice-cold shivers shot through Callan. Why would Patricia want to frame him and destroy his career? They'd had no interaction in the last decade and a half aside from the odd casual greeting. How had he angered her?

Callan pulled up the pictures on his phone and showed them to Hailey. 'Can ye recognise which chain ye worked on?'

Hailey bit her lips and zoomed in. The digital clock in the corner blinked, signalling the late hour.

The night held its breath – no bats, no wind rustling the leaves.

'This one.' Hailey proffered his phone, her shivery voice betraying the exterior calm. 'It's this chain.'

Callan's stomach roiled. They'd found this chain around Fayola's neck.

Which sick bastard got a chain cleaned and re-engraved by a daughter to murder her mother?

'Thank ye.'

Hailey's entire being slouched. 'Anything I can do to help. The handwriting on this other pendant differs from mine.'

She had been of tremendous help already, giving them a lead. But Callan had one more request. This bastard had to have got the second chain done at some place close to town. 'Hailey, can ye ask around in yer circles if someone received a similar chain for engraving and polishing recently?'

She bobbed her head. 'There are a handful of artists hereabouts. I'll call them. This… It still hasn't sunk in for me. And I know it'll get worse. The least I can do is bring whoever did this to justice. Callan…' With trembling hands, Hailey shoved the few strands out of her eyes. 'The chain, when Patricia brought it along, had aged, but she'd cared for it. It surprised me she still had hers. I dumped mine in the bin ages ago.'

Callan nodded. She'd dumped her chain, and he had buried his to symbolise the death of his naivety.

He walked to the door, Aileen in tow.

When the doorknob twisted, he looked over his shoulder at Hailey. 'What business did Fayola have at 46 Wallace Street the day someone abducted Candace Willoughby?'

Hailey frowned. 'Meeting a friend? She isn't into real estate anymore. But she keeps… kept tabs on her co-workers.'

Callan thanked Hailey again and left.

Fayola had been up to something, and they had to know what.

CHAPTER ELEVEN

Patricia had moved to Dachaigh since the police had taken over her house. It would take a couple of days to set everything to rights.

Callan knocked on her door, and it opened a crack. 'Get lost! I have nothing to say to you.'

'Ms Adair.' Callan kept his tone professional. He didn't want another complaint, so he treaded carefully. 'I need to know about the chain.'

With an indignant air, Patricia rolled her eyes at him. 'My friend persuaded me to polish the chain. Clean out the old memories and give it away. I hate uncertainty. *His* disappearance is unresolved – it's unsettling.'

Why not use the dustbin? Callan wanted to ask, but the clock ticked. She'd slam the door in his face soon.

'Why did you get the name "Callan" engraved on it, after removing yours?'

Patricia twiddled her thumbs, refusing to meet his gaze. 'My friend suggested doing that. I felt so guilty. Callan, I-I behaved horribly with you, after what you went through. So I got your name done and gave the chain away.'

Callan raised an eyebrow. 'Where did ye dispose of it?'

'Gave it away.'

'Who suggested you get the name "Callan" engraved on the chain?'

She didn't respond.

Callan bent to Patricia's eyeline. 'Who hurt ye the other night?'

'It's complicated.'

He grew irritated at her crisp answers. He wanted to help her. 'The name, Patricia.'

She shivered. 'Look, I don't know what you want with the chain, but this – this other night was personal. He – he wants cash from me, some money I owe him. I haven't got much left after the cheating bastard emptied our bank account.'

She still hadn't given him the name of this person.

'Please, Ms. Adair. There's been a murder at yer house and we need yer assistance.'

Patricia huffed. 'I don't know why she'd be there. All these questions are giving me a headache. The paramedic told me I need to rest. Goodnight, Detective.'

The door slammed in his face, as he'd predicted. Callan turned to Aileen, who leaned against the wall.

Patricia's reaction worried him. Why the secrecy? And why would she steal her invoice?

Aileen gestured for Callan to follow.

They walked into the kitchen, where she heated up some leftovers. Her back to him, Aileen pulled out a plate and talked. 'Did you see the size of her feet? They're huge. She's a nine easily. No way can she fit into a size seven.'

Callan dug into the food Aileen set in front of him. The spiced spaghetti and mince made his mouth water. 'This's good,' he said with a full mouth.

Aileen chuckled. 'Wow, it's the first time you've commented on my food.'

'I'm hungry.'

Aileen leaned on her elbows. 'Sure.'

Truthfully, he hadn't been eating much. His eyes had sunk in his face, and this case had knackered him. He wouldn't rest until he'd solved it.

'What's the plan now?' Aileen's eyes twinkled with anticipation, excitement.

'Robert'll be looking into Fayola's things. He's already at her house with a forensic team. I'll be there tomorrow. Erm, would ye like to—'

Aileen nodded. 'I want to be there.'

❄

'Looks like being an estate agent pays well,' Aileen muttered to herself.

They stood in a clean neighbourhood where the smallest house had three bedrooms and a porch with a foyer.

'Sure does.'

Side by side they walked towards a maroon door with a brass door knocker. A warm glow emanated from the four windows on the ground floor. Netted curtains hid the inside from view. The white frames were welcoming and had a couple of baubles dangling in the windows.

A blotchy Hailey stood in the doorway.

Her pale disposition contrasted with her reddened eyes and cheeks. 'Morning,' she wheezed, her voice rough from all the sobbing.

Silently, she turned and strode inside. Taking it as an invitation, Callan followed.

Inside, the house appeared as comfy as the exterior.

Long grey sofas sat in a U-shape around a fireplace that crackled even now, thick woollen blankets draped over the sofas' arms. The TV mounted on the other side of the room hissed with the latest news.

A couple of lamps glowed, their golden light sparkling off little ornaments and trinkets placed on the various shelves or tables. Someone had pinned an intricately decorated golden star on the rear wall.

In contrast with the bare walls in Hailey's flat, this house clearly belonged to an artist.

Adelaide hadn't greeted them yet. Callan surveyed the house once again.

Hailey sank into one sofa, bundling herself in a blanket. 'Sorry, Mama's gone out for a walk. She couldn't stand the officials going through Mum's things.' Hailey bit her lip hard, but the tears spilled down her cheeks. 'Sorry, I'm a mess.'

Aileen walked to her and crouched to look into her eyes. 'I can't begin to know the pain you're in. I'm sorry for your loss.'

Hailey buried her head in her hands. 'Please find who did this.'

Callan tapped Aileen on the shoulder and gestured for her to follow him.

They went up the carpeted staircase leading to a landing that forked into four doors. One of them lay wide open.

Sounds of someone tinkering from inside the room met their ears. The other three rooms were silent.

They strode over to the open door to see a pair of legs sticking out from underneath the bed. 'What's so fascinating under the bed, Officer Davis?' Callan asked.

The legs jerked, and there was a bang as his head hit the underside of the bed, followed by a curse.

Muttering more profanities, Robert emerged from under the bed, rubbing the back of his skull.

Aileen stepped ahead, trying to stifle a chuckle, and eyed the vanilla-scented candle by the window. Fayola had been a good interior designer. What could she hide under the bed, though? 'Didn't they teach you to be vigilant in training?'

Callan crossed his arms. 'They do, but some item of high importance under the bed mesmerised Officer Davis. What was this item of significance?'

Robert blinked as if he hadn't understood the question. When Callan glared at him, he looked at his feet and gasped. 'Oh, ye mean— Sorry. I found diaries under the bed. It's strange, innit?'

Aileen ambled over to the closet at the foot of the bed. 'What's strange?' she asked, peering inside. Fayola sure had a knack for fashion. 'This is a large closet!'

Robert hummed. 'Too large for one.'

Callan frowned. 'One? It should be Fayola and Adelaide's.'

'They have separate bedrooms. From what I gathered from the daughter, they never saw eye to eye so they didn't share a bedroom.'

Aileen leaned against the closet door. Their marriage sounded nothing more than a farce.

Callan sighed. 'To each his own, right? There's no point in judging them. If they had a rift, a big enough rift to do with an insurance kitty or infidelity…'

Those were strong motivations for someone to murder their spouse. And based on how Adelaide had treated them last night, she didn't have a kind heart.

Aileen gawked at the closet space. Real estate must pay well.

Callan pulled out his notepad. 'Once Adelaide comes

in, I'll speak with her. Until then, let's go through this room.'

They searched Fayola's closet, especially the personal drawers. Aileen giggled when Callan shuddered and blushed at some contents, despite wearing gloves.

He shot her a glare. 'This isn't funny.'

Oh, but watching awkward Callan made her laugh!

Aileen searched through the drawers for any piece that didn't fit with Fayola's life – letters, knick-knacks, anything exceptional that might have been hidden there – but came up empty-handed.

She reassured Callan when he indicated a set of pointy shoes.

'They can cut through people's feet!' he whispered in horror.

'Are you trying to make me laugh or are you genuinely horrified?'

Callan narrowed his eyes at her. 'This isn't even mildly amusing.'

He pulled out a large box discarded under the many shelves.

Aileen helped him lift the lid and gaped. 'Boots!'

Callan picked a shoe. They were olive green, although now a thick layer of mud covered the once-black sole.

He turned the boot upside down and recognition hit him. 'Ah…'

'What is it?'

'It's a size seven and, as Robert said, has the company's logo imprinted on its sole.'

Fayola Noah had broken into Adelaide's store and stolen an invoice?

'Robert!' He instructed the officer to take the boots into evidence and match them to the print outside Adelaide's shop.

'Callan, what would Fayola want with an invoice?'

'Beats me. It would justify why the burglar didn't tinker with the alarm. Fayola must have had a key. Despite the trouble in paradise, I bet Adelaide kept a spare key hereabouts. All she has to do is walk into the shop, take the invoice and get out. I think she must've run into a desk. That's the noise Hailey heard. So she hurried out without setting the alarm or locking the door.'

Aileen tapped her chin. 'Fayola met Mr Edgar at Blaine's house, then she steals an invoice regarding Patricia's chain and ends up dead?'

Callan eyed the journals Robert had placed in the evidence pile then walked over to them and studied the dust patterns on the leather-bound covers.

Fayola had been rolling in it. Was this a simple case of jealousy, or did it somehow link to Blaine's disappearance?

'Poisoning is a feminine way to kill someone,' he said. 'But it's not that satisfying for a spouse out for vengeance. Let's speak with Adelaide and peek into the family dynamics in this house.'

❄

AILEEN'S FINGERS DANCED ACROSS THE PHONE SCREEN AS the car sped back to the police station. Distracting herself from Callan's driving could keep her anxiety at bay. Despite him being an officer of the law, his driving disconcerted her.

Callan's jaw was clenched so tight it could've smashed his teeth. He held the steering wheel in a death grip as well. 'I need to look into this new guest of yers.'

She hummed, stifling the urge to clench her eyes shut as he manoeuvred round a tight bend.

They hadn't found much from Adelaide, nothing they didn't already know.

Callan's phone shrilled, destroying the tension in the car. Ginny, the owner of the fashion and antique shops in town, spoke without greeting. 'Callan, you need to come see this.'

Aileen and Callan exchanged a look. What could it be?

'Ten minutes.'

Callan put his foot down, urging the car to go full throttle.

They pulled into the police station's parking lot at half-past one. Ginny's shop was a five-minute hike.

A group of teenage girls walked arm in arm, munching on sandwiches, speaking, and giggling all at once. Thanks to the sun, a couple of seniors had stepped out for a stroll. One man with hair as white as snow sat slurping an ice lolly.

The sandwich shop opposite the antique store bustled with schoolkids, the office crowd and those who wanted to grab a bite while running errands.

Ginny's antique store was a relic. The window display exhibited several wooden pieces and the door – a deep, glistening wood – resembled the doors of an Indian fort. The brass knobs glittered under the sun.

Pushing it open, they entered a land of sandalwood.

The atmosphere misted mystically, as if at any moment these artefacts might wither and vanish. Some coins were on display, strategically placed under the beams of tiny lights. There were a few books, their spines cracked to reveal their edition and the author's signature. Smaller stones and art pieces glimmered under the soft golden light overhead.

They'd stepped through time into the Middle Ages.

The beaded curtain at the far end tinkled to reveal a

chic woman with a black bob and perfect eyelashes. Bangles adorned her wrists, clinking as she sauntered towards them. Her wraparound skirt was a deep magenta, making her appear like she danced.

Ginny didn't smile. Instead, she gestured for them to follow her. In her tiny office, she pointed at the seats and retrieved an old box.

'I'm sorry to have dragged you away from your work, but this came to me yesterday. I was far too busy to go through it then so when I did, I had to call you immediately.'

The thin container looked like a shoebox, though it was made of tin. Its edges had rusted with age, and mud stuck to the sides, especially on the edge of the lid. The pictures on it had now faded into splotches of brown and red mixed in with some dark green.

What was this about?

Ginny passed them a pair of gloves each. She placed the spectacles dangling around her neck on her pert nose and clapped the edge of her gloves over her wrists. They snapped, sending her bangles tinkling.

Smoothing out the crumpled paper she'd placed the box on, Ginny pulled the lid open with delicate force. It squeaked, lifting centimetre by centimetre. 'Too much pressure, and I'm afraid it might break. It's an old tin box, the one ye'd get with biscuits and such.'

When she placed the lid aside and sat back, the lamp's light fell on the objects inside.

Callan gaped. 'What the hell!'

Inside the box sat another one, also made of tin.

Curious, Aileen peered at the contents. Callan's face had turned ashen.

What's wrong?

Aileen laid a hand on his thigh and squeezed.

'Breathe, Callan.'

Callan's thigh stiffened for a moment. Then at a snail's pace he followed her instructions, his skin too peaky.

Did he recognise the box? Was it his?

The smaller of the tin boxes would've been blue once upon a time. Such a container could be used to store peppermint or strips of chewing gum.

Callan lifted the tiny box with shivering fingers and, like Ginny had, inched it open. The thing creaked, rickety with age, but no mud or rust coated it.

The lid popped, and Callan tipped the contents into his palm. He knew what it contained. How?

As if on cue, metal clanked and slid into Callan's palm. It was an oxidised chain.

Aileen's heart thundered. 'That's… That's the same chain from before!'

His response sounded hoarse. 'Aye, it is.'

Callan held it up to the light.

A black bird suspended from the chain. Its lustre had faded with age. The simple lettering flashed clearly against the blackened silver: 'Callan'.

How many such chains were there? What importance did they have?

Aileen looked inside the box again and gasped. 'Callan?'

Inside sat a single handkerchief, and an enamelled dagger that had turned ochre with age. The handle had a single brown spot, like a splotch of dried blood. And the handkerchief beside it…

Aileen pulled it out. The brown cloth crackled as it unfolded, crisp in her fingers. Its dark brown shade repulsed her, and an unusual odour tickled Aileen's nostrils. Yuck, what was it?

The rancid odour tugged at her gut.

She undid the rest of the folds. The handkerchief's brown shade didn't appear to be its original colour.

Callan visibly swallowed as he eyed the box and the handkerchief. Finally, he turned to Aileen. 'Dried blood – the handkerchief's coated in dried blood.'

Vomit rose in her throat, and she promptly dropped the item. Who kept such trophies? Was someone declaring another murder?

Aileen placed the knife back in the box and disposed of her gloves. She needed some air if she didn't want to boke on Ginny's expensive carpet, although judging by the look on Callan's face, he needed her.

Ginny wore a grim expression, too.

'Where did you find this, Ginny?'

She took off her gloves and spectacles. Her eyebrows arched as she spoke. 'That's what's odd about it. I received a parcel, wrapped in newspaper and tied with a white thread. Usually people come to me with an old item they've found in their attics. I quote a price if I'm interested. Otherwise I get an artefact I'm sure will get me a good commission, either on loan or I purchase it at an auction for a client.'

Grimacing at the box, her disgust painted on her face, she continued. 'This one? It came wrapped without a note and I found it on the doorstep early yesterday morning.'

Callan lifted an eyebrow, still looking sickly. 'At yer house?'

Ginny shuddered. 'No! Thank God! I would have freaked, considering what's inside. I came in early like I usually do to dust the place and such, and I found it against the back door. They'd placed it there, hidden under the awning.'

Callan stabbed a finger at the door. 'May I take a look?'

When Ginny nodded, Callan regarded the inconspicuous dark wood camouflaging with the surrounding furniture.

The door was old, an antique in itself, with an old wooden lock. And, Aileen observed, it had a thick three-inch frame fitted with a modern alarm clock.

Ginny wrung her hands, noticing Aileen's gaze. 'I have a lot of pricy artefacts, and I can't afford a break in. I've never thought of getting CCTV cameras though.'

Bobbing his head at Ginny's comment, Callan tugged at the door. It groaned under the weight.

Callan assessed the area outside, his broad frame blocking Aileen's view. She admired Ginny's library instead, which comprised many archaeological books and collection catalogues. Auction catalogues sat in a heap by the library on the floor. And, Aileen noted, Ginny held a PhD in Medieval Studies.

The door shut with a resounding thud and Callan stepped back in.

He turned to Ginny. 'So ye didn't see who it was?'

Her black bob swayed. 'I'm sorry. I should have, but I didn't. I was too preoccupied and frankly miffed.'

Aileen raised an eyebrow. 'Miffed?'

'Yes, do you recall I own the apparel store next door? Well, I'd asked Adelaide to refill the dwindling inventory with some custom jewellery pieces. They haven't yet arrived.'

Callan tilted his head. 'What custom jewellery is this?'

Ginny blinked. 'Rings and a couple of pendants.'

Pointing to the smaller tin box, Callan asked, 'Any pendant that looks like this one?'

'No. These are more intricate, feminine designs, custom made to customers' choices.'

Callan thanked Ginny for reporting the box, then

packed the entire tin container, along with its contents, for evidence, and gave Ginny a receipt for it.

'Please don't share this with anyone else. Let's keep it confidential for a while.'

The right side of Ginny's lips twitched in a small smile. 'I'm not from Loch Fuar. Don't worry, I know a bit about confidentiality.'

Once outside, Aileen turned to Callan. 'Are you okay?'

He hummed, but she didn't miss his pensive mood. She let him brood until they entered the air-conditioned police station and sat at his paper-strewn desk with warm mugs of coffee.

'Spill.'

Callan ran a hand through his hair and sighed, shoulders drooping. He set the wrapped box on the table and pointed at it. 'The bluish tin box inside? The smaller one? It's mine.'

Blaine's chain had been with him?

Stunned, Aileen sat mum. This box was Callan's? No, the tiny box belonged to him, not the rest of it!

Of course he'd have a chain too as a member of the White Birds.

But if this chain belonged to him, what was it doing in a tin box that wasn't his?

Muttering a curse, Callan stood and stalked towards the murder board. 'The stranger this case gets, the tighter the noose wraps around this group. Gerald Erwin, Hailey Noah, Jason Mitso, Patricia Adair, and Cosimo Bocelli.'

'Why wasn't it with you?' Aileen mumbled, wary of the answer.

He turned on her, a vein on his forehead throbbing. 'Because Daniel and I buried it fifteen years ago!'

Talk about surprises. This man knew how to keep her on her toes!

Callan had buried the chain instead of binning it. There must be some symbolic meaning behind that. Now wasn't the time for heavy talk though – they had a murderer to catch.

Aileen affixed her sleuthing cap to her head and studied the board.

Callan had spoken to Candace Willoughby, and then someone had attacked her and dumped her in the boot of his car. An ancient car though it was, it worked fine but had suddenly died outside her house.

'Someone tampered with your car. So were they lying in wait? Or had they decided to frame you for this even if you hadn't visited her?'

'Rory told me to visit Candace because she had information to add – she'd phoned in.'

Aileen mulled over Callan's words. Someone had also gone to great lengths to get those pendants made in two separate places. The bloody handkerchief added to the complexity.

She trembled at the thought of that foul item. And the dagger. The dagger's blade gleamed clean. No blood or grime.

Callan sank into his chair, the heavy pouches under his eyes speaking of sleepless nights.

'What was I thinking, being friends with these people? One or all of them knows a secret about Blaine and they want it hidden.'

Yes, they did. But what secret did they want to hide?

It troubled her, how defeated Callan sounded. She thought back to what he'd said about his chain. He and *Daniel* had buried.

And he'd also told her that Candace had mentioned Blaine had fought with the handyman.

Twirling a lock of hair, she thought about it.

Handyman.

Daniel was a handyman, but never one to throw punches at someone half his size.

'Have you spoken to Daniel about this?'

He scorched her with a glare. 'Do I look like an eejit to point the blame at someone who's never let me down?'

Men could surely be thick sometimes. Aileen took matters into her hands. At least they could resolve the issues in their control.

She pointed at Callan. 'Meet me by the car in ten minutes.'

CHAPTER TWELVE

Daniel McIntyre gaped at her straightforward question.

Dressed in jeans and a plaid shirt, his hair stuck out in all angles. He held his bairn on his right hip.

'Why would I argue with Blaine over Callan? I'd never hurt him. If I had an issue with Callan, I'd punch the sod. I won't say I've never brawled; I have, but I'd never bully anyone.'

He grimaced when Carly drooled on his shirt. His lips twisted into a loving smile as he kissed her strawberry blond curls.

'I stood larger than most lads my age, never a tiny child. The first thing my paw instilled in me was to be respectful of people. Callan and I, especially as lads, we enjoyed throwing punches at each other. It's how we communicated until he—' He cleared his throat. 'No, I never hurt a hair on Blaine's head. What makes ye ask if I did?'

Aileen hung her head. She'd been a fool to be so direct, yet she had to, for Callan's sake. This case was beating down on him enough without the added stress of looking at Daniel as a suspect. 'Callan would never ask, and I wanted to ensure he never has doubts about you or your friendship.'

Daniel pursed his lips. 'Aye, if I had a beef with Callan, I'd sock him in the face. I know he'd fight back. It's the most efficient way to resolve issues, but I'd never punch someone half my size.'

Words were better, she thought. At least they didn't mean a trip to the hospital. Hateful tongues, though, surely hurt way longer than a physical bruise.

She bobbed her head. 'Thanks, Daniel, and I'm sorry.'

'Sure thing.'

'Hey.' She paused on her way out. 'If you ever get the chance, tell Callan what you told me, and please sock him in the face. It might make him feel better.'

Daniel grinned. 'Will do.'

❄

CALLAN RAISED AN EYEBROW WHEN THE WHITEWASHED INN with its cheery flowers came into view. The pastel-blue window frames were wide open to welcome the fresh summer air.

Aileen tilted her head. 'What?'

'Where did ye go?'

'Personal business.'

Her tone sounded too smart, which clued him in on the possibility she was up to some mischief.

She'd spritzed her citrus perfume this morning, and in the confines of the car, it played with his mind and heart.

They strode over to the front door, and the aromatic scent of cinnamon made his stomach protest.

Aileen hooted with laughter. 'Is there a GPS in your stomach? Anytime you're near a kitchen, it growls.'

His scowl had her guffawing right there in the reception area.

Five minutes later, Callan sat at the kitchen counter, enjoying some leftover snacks and coffee.

Aileen leaned her elbows on the marble, too engrossed in her phone.

'Where has your Mr Edgar gone to?' Callan grumbled, swallowing the last piece of his pie.

'I saw him yesterday heading towards Fayola's old office. It was the same afternoon she died.'

Callan licked the crumbs from his lips. The pie was too good to wipe the extra bits. Damn manners.

When he sat silently for a while, Aileen looked up from her phone. 'What is it?'

Wasn't it obvious?

Fayola couldn't entertain him from the coroner's, could she? If he hadn't returned to the inn after his jaunt into town, he could've run away.

'I need his data now.'

Aileen shook her head. 'Can't give it to you without a warrant. But,' – she held up her hand and peered at the sprawling Highlands, a perfect backdrop for this homely kitchen. 'His car is still here. He never leaves without his car for the entire day.'

'Why?'

'He limps. I reckon it's either diabetes or arthritis.'

Callan leaned a hip against the kitchen counter. 'Ye must have some documents about this man. Ye said he gave ye a driving licence. Show it to me please.'

She tsked. 'I'll need a warrant to let you go through my documents, Detective Cameron. Although there's this thing needing my attention in the larder. Room 7.' She hissed the last bit and sauntered off, whistling to herself.

What a woman…

He stalked towards the reception area.

Being technologically handicapped, Callan spewed swear words like an endless rhyme. He clicked the poor mouse so many times it got stuck on repeat.

Eventually, he found a menu with a list of each guest and their room number. He scrolled to Room 7 and clicked through.

It took a while for the image to load, but once it did, Callan peered at the tiny image in the corner of the screen.

'Bloody hell! Bollocks!' his voice boomed through the inn.

Footsteps thundered towards him, and Aileen burst into the reception area. 'Callan! You scared me. What is it?'

Her dark brown hair had escaped her ponytail. Aileen held a duster in one hand and a cleaning spray in the other. She'd stuffed her hands in large yellow gloves.

'Don't ye have housekeeping staff?'

'What?'

Never mind.

Callan pointed at the computer screen. 'This isn't Mr Matthew Edgar.'

Aileen's face went pale. 'What? Not again!' She groaned. 'I checked him out and his licence looked legitimate.'

She plodded around the counter and stared at the picture.

He pointed at the gruff face. 'I'd recognise this man anywhere. This is Matthew Macgregor. This is Blaine's father.'

Matthew Macgregor hadn't had the white hair or wrinkles fifteen years ago, but that dissatisfied scowl and sneer on his face? He was Blaine's father, alright. Damn it! Callan should have checked him out sooner.

Callan reached for his phone, dialling. They needed to track him down. 'For all we ken, he murdered his son and is here to bury the bloody clues.'

❄

CALLAN'S SHOULDER RUBBED AGAINST AILEEN'S AS THEY both hunkered in the Control Room and navigated through the surveillance footage.

'Thank God I got this installed. Lesson learned, yet I got fooled again.'

He reached for her soft hand and gave it a squeeze. 'It's an authentic licence, Aileen. Stop beating yerself up.'

Callan had little hope that the footage would give them major clues, but he would take anything he could get.

The footage from the morning popped onto the screen. A couple of families left the inn, laughing and chatting, set to enjoy their day.

It had been a pleasant one so far, with crisp air and welcoming grass. Rightly so, most tourists dressed for a hike.

When the clock struck half past ten, Matthew Edgar, aka Macgregor, stepped out. At least he hadn't been fibbing about his limp.

At a slow pace, he limped out of sight of the footage.

Aileen pointed at him as he disappeared from the screen. 'See this? He turns towards the road and not towards his car. I wonder who picked him up.' She turned to Callan and shivered. 'I hope they didn't kidnap him – or worse.'

Callan hoped so, too.

Aileen gripped his arm. 'What can I do?'

'Look at why he switched names. Figure out what happened to Matthew Macgregor and the wife, Blaine's mother. To my knowledge, she's passed, but ye might as well clarify. And also check property records if ye can.'

'Roger that.'

Scepticism tugged at his gut. 'Aileen? Do not – I repeat, do not – go following up on any suspects or anything that catches yer fancy either by yerself or with Isla or anyone else. Whatever ye want to look into, ye tell me and we'll look into it together. Am I clear?'

She shot him a glare, but conceded.

It was time to reacquaint himself with Matthew Macgregor.

❄

THE CLOCK CHIMED A QUARTER AFTER MIDNIGHT. CALLAN made it back to his office and collapsed into his chair, groaning at the strain. His head throbbed, as did his right knee.

Damn it!

He'd spoken to everyone: Isla, Barbara who ran the tea shop, and he'd also visited the pub. Callan and Robert had even gone to Blaine's old house, although without a warrant, they couldn't enter. He'd driven past his suspect's houses only to notice nothing untoward.

Finally, Robert had gone through the highway surveillance. Since they wouldn't know if Macgregor had stolen a car, their searched ended up futile. His car was still parked at Dachaigh.

Rory had taken over the task of getting a warrant from the judge. Given the late hour, Callan didn't expect it to come through until the morning. And without proof, Macgregor wasn't a suspect either.

Callan let his head fall back and shut his eyes.

Rory knocked on the door. His face appeared grim. 'The warrant's under process.'

Dread sunk into the pit of his stomach. 'Ye look knackered.'

His boss sank into the visitor's chair and rubbed his face. 'Willoughby's registered the complaint with the Chief Constable and it's being forwarded to the PSD. They'll send an officer to investigate the case. I'm sorry, Callan.'

He was sorry, too. Sorry the system he'd worked so hard for had bitten him. He hadn't done anything wrong, had he? If this investigating officer couldn't peg this case, Callan would.

He nodded. 'Thanks for giving me a heads-up.'

'Sure thing. See ye tomorrow.'

Callan huffed. What unwelcome surprises and challenges would tomorrow bring?

❄

AILEEN HAD OUTSOURCED THE BIT ABOUT PROPERTY records to a more resourceful individual, aka Isla. And according to Isla's early morning message, the Macgregors had sold their house fourteen years ago to Edgar Holdings Pvt Ltd.

Edgar Holdings Pvt Ltd was a dormant company created fifteen years ago solely to purchase Blaine's house by the look of it.

Why would Macgregor create a separate company?

Aileen had combed through all the data she could find on this man.

As Callan had informed her, Mrs Macgregor had died about five years ago. She had been ill for a long time.

When she dug into it further, she deciphered Mrs Macgregor's Asian family came from money. It could be one reason the Macgregors hadn't sold their old house to buy another in Inverness.

Since his wife had passed, and the flow of money had apparently been cut off, Mr Macgregor needed funds. And selling the house would give him a leg-up.

She'd texted Callan before dawn, asking if they'd found Matthew Macgregor. This time he'd responded but with negative news. There was still no sign of him.

The warrant hadn't come through yet either.

Aileen was arranging some leftovers in a container when a car rumbled to a halt outside. The back door opened and a red-haired ball of energy gushed in, her green eyes wide. 'Still no sign of Macgregor?'

'No, he's disappeared like Houdini.'

Isla hummed and leaned a hip on the counter as Aileen worked. 'Say, Aileen, he didn't take his car along, did he?'

'They would've easily caught him if he had.'

Unlike herself, Isla sat quietly for a long moment. 'Say, what if he took another car?'

Aileen wiped the table, dumping some vegetable peelings in the bin. 'The police think so – or someone could've abducted him.'

Isla gripped the marbled counter. 'What if he took Fayola's car?'

'Huh?' She looked at Isla, focusing on what she'd just said.

Isla's eyes were twinkling now. 'I heard Fayola had gone to a yoga retreat. So she'd have taken her car. Where is it? Did you see it at her house or at the shop?'

Aileen hadn't seen Fayola's car. She had to have had one. What other way could she get about town? The bus service ran infrequently, and it seemed unlikely she'd have sold the one she'd have used for work – particularly given the fiery relationship with her wife. Aileen couldn't see them sharing a car when they couldn't even share a bedroom.

'I didn't think about this. I'll have to ask Callan.'

Isla's eyes lit with naughtiness. 'So you two are back together, eh?'

She didn't want to add fuel to the gossip mill; nor did she want to tip her gran off. Aileen sighed. 'Solving the case together since we gathered some pertinent info.'

Green eyes scrutinised her, but Isla didn't pry. 'I can see the smirk. You made up. Or out.' She wiggled her eyebrows.

Aileen's cheeks heated. 'I-I'll head to the police station.'

❄

AILEEN CARRIED TWO STEAMING TO-GO CUPS AND A BAG OF sugary pastries to Callan's office.

The grumpy man slumped in his chair, eyes closed and snoring. She suppressed a giggle at the drool on his chin.

Placing their breakfast on his messy desk, she tiptoed behind the chair and poked him in the ribs.

It was a bad idea. Callan immediately lunged and had her pinned before she could so much as blink.

'Callan, it's me!' She squirmed.

A muttered curse tickled her ears. 'Ever heard of knocking?'

Straightening her shirt, Aileen fingered the hem. 'You were snoring.'

'Was not!' Callan sniffed. 'Where's the coffee?'

'Well, good morning to you, too. And you're welcome.'

He snatched the go-cup from the tray. The coffee woke him like firecrackers on a silent night and softened the grumpiness his face held. And with it, the puffiness of sleep vanished.

'Why did you spend the night in a chair?'

Callan swallowed and gestured to the other bag she'd brought. She took out a small plastic box. 'I brought you some leftovers. They're still warm if you—'

'Thank ye. If I'd have kent complimenting ye would make ye want to cook for me, I'd've commented on yer cooking a while ago.'

Aileen rolled her eyes. He had deftly ignored her question. She asked again, 'Why'd you spend the night here?'

Callan huffed. 'The Willoughbys have registered their complaint. And the PSD will send an investigative officer over soon. And if that's not enough pressure, we searched into the wee hours for Macgregor.'

She tapped her chin. 'Well… Isla asked if he'd maybe taken Fayola's car?'

Callan jumped in his seat and stared at Aileen as if she'd grown horns. 'Why the bloody hell didn't I think of that before? Robert!'

Hurried footsteps answered his bellow. Robert grinned at Aileen. 'Hey!'

'Contact Adelaide Noah or her daughter. Ask if they know where Fayola's car is.'

'Cool.' Robert tapped his forehead. 'We got a call from forensics. They can't peg the blood on the knife yet but they've sent you detailed pictures of all the items.'

Callan's grin appeared like he was gnashing his teeth. 'I'll look into them, see if anything pops.'

He pulled up the images as Aileen scraped a chair over to his side of the desk.

Heads touching, they studied the images.

The enamelled knife looked the same except for the tag hanging from it. They had also tagged the handkerchief and chains.

'Do you think this links to the case?' Aileen tilted her head, lips inches away from Callan's. What had she been doing?

His gaze faltered, breaking the brief spell. 'Dinnae ken, but we've got nothing else to look into until Robert gets back to us. And I hate coincidences. If a sinister item like this turns up at Ginny's antique shop the same day as Fayola's murder, we need to look into it. Let's cover our bases.'

That much was true.

Callan first zoomed into the image of his old chain.

They studied the metal, yet all he saw were the chipped areas and scratches.

Next came the handkerchief, but apart from the dried blood, they found nothing of significance on it. Blood soaked the fibres, yet the thing seemed mundane, with no embossing or any pattern that stood out.

He brought the dagger up next.

They zoomed in on the enamelled hilt. It glistened under the light. With hope in their eyes, they took their time studying the piece, but the curved design offered nothing to identify its owner.

How old could it be? Early twentieth century at the minimum. They should've asked Ginny.

Callan harrumphed. 'Now what?'

Aileen tsked. What happened to doing a thorough job? 'Let's study the entire thing. There might be inscriptions on the blade.'

Taking control of the laptop, she scrolled down to the blade.

The plain metal glinted with a sharp edge. They studied it from top to bottom, and when they reached the tip, an exclamation slipped through Aileen's lips.

'What's that?'

'Looks like a coat of arms of sorts.' Head tilted, Aileen bit her lip as she traced the symbol. Two thistles curved around a sceptre. 'It's engraved on the blade. No name or words.'

She let him study it. 'I'll search for it online.'

Robert's knock on the door interrupted them. 'Sorry to disturb you, but the Noahs confirmed they dinnae ken where Fayola's car is.'

'Ah hell!'

Wide-eyed, Aileen stared between Robert and Callan. They stood gaping at each other. What were they waiting for?

'Well, move!'

Robert shook his head. 'We don't know where her car is and I'm certain I didn't see it on the surveillance footage.'

How could these men be just in their thirties? The Loch Fuar team needed a seminar on technology.

If the car belonged to Fayola, it had to be a fancy top model. And so did her phone.

'Get me her phone, Robert.'

❄

AILEEN HAD SCOURED THE INTERNET FOR A HIT ON THE coat of arms and found nothing like it anywhere.

Thistles were Scottish wildflowers, and the sceptre used by royalty. Who in Loch Fuar belonged to Scottish royalty?

Huffing, Aileen checked the time. It was four in the afternoon now. 'I think I'll go meet Ginny and ask her about this.'

'Sure. Help us track Fayola's car first.'

It took Robert another half an hour to fetch the phone.

Callan breathed down her right shoulder and Robert on her left. Despite the several attempts at shoving them away, they didn't budge.

Aileen licked her lips. The tech team had unlocked the phone.

She tapped on the icon she wanted. 'This app will help us locate her car.'

Callan cursed. 'Damn technology.'

Technology was useful. Aileen grinned as the app searched.

It buffered for a while and then pinged.

Aileen threw her hands up, her head back. 'Found it!'

Callan snatched the phone from her hands. 'Where?'

Eager much?

'Bloody hell! Why didn't I think about this before? He's at the post office – or rather the rental flat above the post office!'

❄

Callan stood in the silent street behind the post office, studying the scene before he began to stalk towards the building.

Fayola's phone guided him onwards, the icon barely moving forward as he walked.

Adrenaline pumped into his blood. What if Macgregor was their man? What if he'd killed his son?

Callan swallowed his melancholy.

Eyes out for the car, Cameron!

When the app didn't beep and he couldn't see any fancy cars parked in the street, Callan almost lost hope. He approached the post office's back door, wondering if he should turn back. Even technology goofed up sometimes.

But then he saw it, tucked behind a large skip: a car covered in a plastic sheet. Fayola's phone beeped in his pocket.

Found it!

Crouching in front of the vehicle, Callan lifted the sheet and read the licence plate. It was Fayola's alright.

A spiral staircase led to the inconspicuous flat above the tiny post office. Despite the fact that there was still plenty of daylight, someone had drawn the curtains.

Callan made his way up the stairs; the misty afternoon drizzle had made the ironwork slippery, but the friction slits kept him from having an accident.

Soon he stood at the brown door.

From inside the flat, the crackle of a TV sounded. Someone was enjoying a relaxing afternoon.

His two raps were like smacks on an anvil.

A loud silence followed, and Callan knocked again – harder.

Water dripped from the awning above the door and landed on his shoulder. Callan swatted it away.

A few moments later, grunting followed heavy treads, the locks clicked and the door unlatched.

Ah, finally.

The man hadn't changed. He was as stout as he'd always been, his mouth still holding the same sneer, although his thinning hair had gone white and a prickly stubble marred his jaw.

'Hello, Mr Macgregor. It's nice to meet ye again.'

Matthew Macgregor sighed. 'I see ye found me.'

Callan plucked his badge to show him. 'We need ye to come to the station and answer a few questions.'

A dark shadow fell on his face. 'So ye're a detective now, eh?' He appraised Callan. 'I need my coat, and then I'll be right along. I'm ready to talk.'

CHAPTER THIRTEEN

The plastic folder snapped on the table, and the chair screeched when Callan pulled it back. He steepled his fingers and gave the other man a long look. 'Mr Matthew Macgregor.'

Perspiration beaded on the man's forehead and upper lip, thanks to the stuffy room. 'Edgar – it's Matthew Edgar.'

Callan tilted his head. 'Why the name change?'

The man narrowed his eyes until they were mere slits. He'd used this trick on Blaine a few times – Callan had heard the tales. 'I can do whatever the hell I want.'

'Including murdering yer son?'

Edgar banged his hands on the table and spat. 'How. Dare. Ye! I would never kill my lad.'

Callan furrowed his brows. 'Why?'

Clasping his hands together as if in prayer, he shook his head. 'Every father and son have their spats. They don't end in murder.'

Edgar's musky cologne made Callan want to gag.

Callan didn't have time to beat around the bush. He wanted straight answers. The only way to get them was to ask straight questions. Leaning in, he mimicked Edgar's pose. 'So tell me, why did ye leave Loch Fuar?'

The old man stared at his fingers. 'We needed a change – of scenery and of life. My wife and I decided to start afresh.'

'Didn't ye ever think yer son would come back looking for ye?'

The older man slapped his hands on the table, rattling it. 'The boy was a feartie running away like he did, leaving his poor mother worried. She got sick because of him. He's dead to me.'

For a man who'd bullied his own son, calling him a coward sounded ironic. Callan stopped himself from rolling his eyes. 'Didn't ye wonder what might have happened to him?'

A muscle in Edgar's brow twitched. He hissed in a low tone, 'We had a spat that day. The lad had a good brain on his shoulders, and what did he want to do? Waste it by playing the damned piano!'

'As far as I ken, the entire world was in awe of Mozart when he composed music aged five. He had a marvellous brain.'

'I don't care about bloody Mozart! Blaine would have made a decent living as a doctor, not trotting around the country playing pianos and starving.'

Callan switched topics. 'What are ye doing here?'

'Selling the blasted house. Why else would I ever come back?' Scowling, the man glowered at Callan.

To search for your lost son or bury clues.

He ignored the man's expression and pressed. 'Why do ye want to sell the place?'

'Money, why else? My wife was seriously ill, and I left

my job to care for her. I didn't have much in the way of resources and did my best to provide for my son, ungrateful eejit that he was. But he blew it all on piano lessons.'

Crossing his legs, Callan paused and waited for more sweat to crowd the older man's creased forehead.

The clock ticked loudly in the room, rattling the older gent. Edgar gulped.

Seeing a chance, Callan went for the blow. 'What was Fayola doing for ye?'

The sneer evaporated, leaving behind fear. His eyes found Callan's. 'I didn't kill her.'

'What's her car doing with ye, then?'

Hands trembling, Edgar shook his head. 'Look, we were selling the house. She had a set of keys and one day, she said she'd found Blaine. I told her I didn't care, but she was having none of it. Then she drove to the inn and asked me to take her into town. I asked why, but she wouldn't say. I dropped her off at the market square where she handed me her car keys. We made plans to meet later. She promised she'd explain it all to me.'

Fayola had found Blaine? Dead or alive?

Callan's eyes were flat as he asked, 'When was this?'

Edgar whispered so low, Callan barely caught the words. 'The afternoon she died.'

'Where were ye going to meet?'

'Behind the post office, although I waited in her old office for a bit.' His eyes pleading with Callan's, the wrinkles on the old man's forehead deepened. 'She told me she'd found a parcel. It was the key, she said, this parcel. She'd found it in the house. I told her I just wanted to sell the place. She never came to meet me like we'd planned in the evening.'

A feartie if he'd ever seen one. Only cowards were this

volatile. 'So when ye heard someone'd killed her, ye thought that person would be after ye too, and thus ye left Dachaigh for the rental flat.'

Edgar ran a hand through his white mop. 'I wanted the money for the house, then I would disappear. I didn't want any part of this mess. As luck would have it, I'd driven halfway to Loch Fuar when ye called. I figured if I stayed out of touch with the locals nobody'd recognise me.'

Uncrossing his legs, Callan sighed. 'Did ye have any offers?'

Edgar snorted. 'One. Fayola said she'd handle the business side of things for me. I just had to sign the papers. She'd be discreet, so I'd agreed to pay her more to get the job done. She'd come out of retirement for me.'

'Did she say who the buyer was?' Callan sat on the brink of losing patience and wanted to punch a wall when the other man shook his head.

'She died before she could tell me.'

❄

GINNY'S CHIC BOB DANCED AROUND HER PRETTY FACE, giving flight to her sandalwood fragrance. 'Sorry, I haven't seen such a symbol before either.'

All hope in Aileen's heart deflated. If Ginny didn't know, who else would?

Aileen took her phone back and stared at the thistles and sceptre.

Ginny pointed at the image. 'It's a common sceptre. I mean, there's no detailing on it – it's too tiny.'

If she'd come to a dead end, it wouldn't pertain to this case, she hoped. Then again, blood covered the handkerchief. Whose blood was it? Whose hand had drawn it?

Too many questions…

Ginny's bangles clanked when she jostled in her seat. 'Why don't you ask your friend Charles Wyatt?'

Charles Wyatt, a revered collector, had helped her in the first case she'd solved. And in turn, she'd helped him out.

She could write to him. Yes, if anyone knew what this symbol meant, he would.

❄

THE MEDICAL EXAMINER'S CALL CAME AFTER SUNSET, AN hour after Callan's shift had ended.

He didn't have time to waste, so he swivelled his car and parked it in front of the ME's office. He wanted as much information as he could get.

The doctor greeted him with a stoic face. She was a middle-aged woman, brilliant at her work.

'I would judge the time of death to be somewhere between 1 and 4 p.m., give or take half an hour. By the foaming, it's poison. I can't tell if she was drugged too, not until the toxicology report comes in. I've found no scrapes and bruises to hint at a tussle; nor is there any DNA on her body or in between her fingernails. No wounds either.'

She didn't beat about the bush, and Callan respected her for it.

He crossed his arms. 'How do ye think the killer administered the poison?'

The doctor pulled out a file, pointing at her report as she read. 'There are two bruises consistent with the use of syringes on her arm.'

The doctor leaned on her elbows. 'My opinion, based on the findings, is she likely died of cyanide poisoning. But

I also think her killer administered a drug to make her compliant. Hence no bruises.'

'Poisoned in a stranger's house? And there's no history of drug abuse for either of them.'

'Looking into suspects is your field of expertise, Detective.'

Most people didn't have syringes lying around; nor did they know how to inject poison, but drugs... A lead to look into.

'Why twice? Why prick her twice?'

'They mightn't have pumped enough into her the first time, or she didn't die instantly. Like I said, perhaps the first was to inject a drug and the second the poison. It's hard to tell without a toxicology report.'

They were either looking for a consummate murderer or a drug addict. Callan had to do the dirty and dig into his former friends' lives.

He sipped coffee that burned his throat. His mind had exploded like live volcanoes erupting every two minutes.

The police databases had records of a couple of his former pals.

Jason Mitso had seen jail walls after brawling in a London pub. And the system had Patricia's fingerprints after she'd thrown a glass vase at her former husband's head.

As for the rest of them? Squeaky clean.

Blast!

Gerald Erwin had too many accolades. He knew how to poke a syringe, but the man, according to Callan's headache-inducing research into medical journals, seemed saint-like. He ought to be nominated for a Nobel prize.

Bleary-eyed, Callan scrolled through Cosimo Bocelli's criminal record. This man didn't pretend to be a stuck-up bastard. He'd been on the bad side of the law a couple of times, especially for trading drugs.

The police had arrested Cosimo Bocelli once for possession. They had also confiscated syringes. It might've been a catalyst for his divorce.

Did Jason know how to use a needle, being friends with Cosimo?

Callan rubbed his tired eyes. He needed to confront Cosimo and determine if he still used.

Why prick Fayola twice? Was the first dose insufficient, as the medical examiner had suggested, or had the murderer been unsure how much she'd needed to die?

He walked to his murder board. Either of these men could have entered Patricia's house with Fayola unnoticed and done the deed.

How had they convinced Fayola to enter Patricia's house, though? And how could they know Patricia wouldn't walk in on them?

This person assumed things would work out. Haughty. Otherwise they wouldn't have written him a letter.

Confidence and deceit.

If the same person had assaulted Candace Willoughby, it took guts to abduct a woman in broad daylight in a tight-knit community.

He thought about the cocky grin Cosimo wore.

Did he just have that kind of confidence in himself, or had he done dirty work like this before?

❄

AILEEN RUBBED HER PALMS TOGETHER FOR WARMTH WITH fleeting comfort. Her fingers tingled numb when the frigid wind weaved through.

Tempted, Aileen had headed over to Blaine's house after meeting with Ginny.

Bad idea!

The house held no more clues.

The sounds of her boots hitting the pavement echoed in the misty afternoon, the wind using the street as its playground and swirling the mist like a witch's potion.

Aileen tucked the straps of her backpack close and strode ahead. The sooner she got to her car, which she'd parked a couple of streets away, the sooner she'd be out of this nightmare.

When the icy wind picked up, causing her to break out in goosebumps, she wanted to run. But the street was covered in slippery puddles and unruly cobblestones, hazards that could trip her. She couldn't chance a fall, not with no one about.

She'd left the cluster of houses behind. The houses here were far apart and faced the silent woods.

Aileen hunkered against the wind and pushed on, blood pounding in her ears.

So deep in deliberation was she, Aileen never realised another pair of footsteps had joined hers.

The footsteps neared, jolting Aileen out of her thoughts, and she gave the other person room to pass. Whoever they were, they were in a hurry, no doubt wanting to get out of this blasted weather.

A shadow loomed over her. It had to be someone tall if their strides could swallow the distance so quickly.

Aileen turned her head in greeting, watching her own footsteps, when suddenly she was grabbed in an iron-like hold.

'Ah!' She fought, her throat closing up, cutting off her oxygen supply.

Her assailant grabbed her backpack and tugged. Since she had both straps on, Aileen tumbled backwards with the bag.

Oh crap! Why was this happening to her? And in Loch Fuar of all places?

Velvety soft hands pushed her while yanking at her bag.

Golly, did he want her wallet?

Shivering, Aileen peeled the backpack off. She didn't carry a lot of cash with her anyway, and she could always cancel her credit cards. No amount of money equalled her life.

She shoved the man, yet he persisted, now grabbing her shirt.

No!

Musk zapped up her nostrils.

Come on, Aileen!

She heard Callan's reprimands in her head from their self-defence sessions, and her training kicked in.

Aileen manoeuvred as Callan had taught her, counting the steps in her head. One, two, three, and she pushed off her feet. Aileen's head crashed against her assailant.

Crack!

'Oof!' Their grip loosened.

Aileen tried steadying herself when her foot caught on a stone and she tumbled to her knees, scraping them raw.

'Ouch!'

Bloody cobblestones! She rubbed her throbbing thigh as bile rose in her throat.

In her frenzy, her backpack slipped from her shoulders, one of its straps broken.

Her assailant grabbed at it again and shoved it away from them.

Aileen lunged for it, but vice-like hands gripped her

shoulders, lifting her off the ground as if she weighed no more than a piece of paper.

She thrashed, using every trick in her limited toolbox, but nothing worked.

Her elbow landed in the person's gut. Another grunt, but it didn't impact her attacker. The person pushed her the other way towards the kerb.

'Ouch!' She crashed to the ground, her previously broken arm crunching underneath her.

No! She wouldn't succumb like a weakling! She would fight this – fight this person!

She saw the person pluck her backpack from where it lay in a soggy puddle and pushed off the ground.

She screeched, terrified, 'Get away!' Her words echoed loudly enough to draw attention. But not a soul loitered on the street.

The assailant dropped her bag and ran off.

Not a moment later, the mist swallowed their silhouette in a large gulp.

'Crap. Dammit.'

Her pants puffed out in smoky clouds and became a part of the mist. She had the sniffles, her heart chugging like an unstoppable drum.

With shaky hands, she grabbed her bag, her body quaking like an earthquake's tremor. Was it from the shock or the cold?

Not giving a damn about the puddles or the cobbled street, she dashed towards her car.

❄

She had to turn her keys a couple of times while warring with hysteria.

Despite the brave face she'd put on, she didn't have the guts to drive to Dachaigh and sit alone in her chambers.

When she parked in front of the police station, Aileen told herself her car had a mind of its own. Involuntarily, her heart clenched at not finding Callan's vehicle in its customary spot.

He hadn't got his SUV back, had he?

She huffed and hurried out of her car towards the door.

Never had she been so glad to smell the coffee scent that always hung in the air. And never had she been so relieved to see the golden glow illuminating the worn carpet outside Callan's door.

Striding towards his office, Aileen contemplated turning around. This was silly. She was behaving like a damsel in distress, running to Callan for help.

She paused next to the coffee machine in the waiting room, her huffing and puffing echoing in the quietness.

Biting her lip, she reconsidered. She'd better head to Dachaigh and call it a day.

Aileen turned around when a gruff voice stopped her. 'Aileen?'

She clutched the backpack to her chest; the bloody strap had come loose. Her favourite bag!

'What is it?' Callan sounded *concerned.*

His heavy footsteps treaded on the carpet.

One look at her and his eyes grew dark. But he didn't say a word. Instead, with a gentleness she'd never thought he possessed, he led her across the room and sat her down on a chair. The next moment, the coffee machine hummed to life.

Another minute and he crouched in front of her with a warm cup and met her gaze. 'Are ye hurt?'

Aileen hissed, looking away. 'No.'

He sighed, cupping her frigid fingers around the warm mug. His actions sent goosebumps erupting over her skin – welcome goosebumps.

Aileen blushed.

Callan's thumb caressed the back of her hand, drawing a blazing trail. Her heart picked up speed for an entirely different reason. Desperate to break this dangerous trance, she stuttered, 'T-Thank you.'

Aileen tucked a loose strand of hair tickling her cheek behind her ear. Their connection broke, the loss tangible.

Callan sat back on his haunches, his hands still wrapped around hers. 'Can ye tell me what happened?'

Aileen told him everything.

With every sentence, Callan's eyes grew darker and his jaw clenched harder. He gripped the handle of the seat so tight, his knuckles turned white.

She hadn't meant to distress him and certainly not anger him. The last thing she needed was a reprimand. She had no energy.

To her surprise, Callan didn't say a word. Instead, he stood and paced. 'Who knew yer whereabouts?'

Aileen huffed. 'No one. I headed over there on a whim.'

His boots echoed in the empty room. 'So they had to be following ye. Was it a man or a woman?'

'It could've been someone random – a mugging?'

Callan swivelled. 'Man or a woman?'

Aileen thought back to the tall silhouette, the musky cologne, and the straight cut of the coat. 'Man.'

He towered over her and gritted out the next question. 'Did ye see what he wore?'

'No.'

Callan plucked the empty mug from her hands and set it aside, then sank into the chair next to hers, taking her hands in his calloused ones once more. 'Close yer eyes and imagine the scene.'

Aileen chuckled. 'This isn't some movie I watched. Someone tried to mug me!' Her voice rose an octave.

His calming blue orbs held hers steadily. 'Go back to the scene, Aileen. Shut yer eyes. What's the weather like?'

'Misty. My hands were freezing.' She shivered at the mere thought.

Callan coaxed in a soothing tone, 'Alright, what can ye hear?'

'The sound of my footsteps followed by another's.' Aileen's heart raced like a sports car on a free road. 'This person walked in a hurry and I thought... He grabbed me.'

Callan rubbed his thumb over the backs of her hands. 'Did he grab ye from behind?'

Aileen nodded.

'Was he wearing gloves?'

She gasped, her mouth forming an O. 'Yes, they were velvety soft, and he wore a black leather coat over a T-shirt, also black.'

Aileen opened her eyes excitedly and blinked at Callan's proximity. His woody scent calmed her accelerating heart.

'Close yer eyes – we aren't done.'

Now encouraged by her success, Aileen tried again. He didn't need to coax her now; the words flowed as she ran him through the event.

'He tugged at my backpack and when it didn't fall off my shoulders, he tried shoving me away.'

Callan leaned on his elbows. 'And ye say he pushed ye to the kerb and shoved yer bag to the other side?'

Aileen thought it out for a moment. 'Not exactly,' she said at last. 'I mean, he tried tugging my bag first. I thought, *My life's more important than money*, so I let him pull it off, but it caught on my shirt, I guess. And then I fought him how you taught me to.' She smiled at him. 'Thanks for teaching me.'

He hissed. 'Ye shouldn't have to use it, Aileen.'

'It saved me.'

Callan's forehead scrunched. 'Did he run away after?'

'No, I fell.'

Callan rolled his eyes, but his gaze fell to her knees. 'Ye've scraped yer knees.'

'I know, sorry. Back to the point. He kicked my bag away and picked me off the ground then shoved me towards the kerb. He got my bag from the other side. I sat up, shouting. My shouts alarmed him, so he dropped it and ran off.'

Eyebrows knitted together, Callan focused on plucking antiseptic and bandages from the first aid kit. 'Did he lift yer bag or did he go through it?'

She'd been lying on the ground, fighting to get through the first ever mugging of her life! How could she remember? For Callan's sake, she tried.

Shutting her eyes again, Aileen visualised the scene. 'Um, my bag was closed. He plucked it off the ground and… Yeah, he faced away from me. I couldn't see what he did with it, yet… Ouch, Callan, it stings…'

'Focus on the story.'

'Easier said than done. Ouch, okay… I remember he wore a lighter shade of shoes – suede I think they were – without a speck of mud on them.'

Her eyes glittered when she opened them. 'It's fantastic how this technique works, Callan!'

He waved a dismissive hand, the frown on his face indicating his mind churned, thinking or concentrating on her injured knee. He tilted his head and pointed at her bag. 'Was it closed when ye found it or open?'

Aileen stared at the poor bag. It had accompanied her on two adventures now, not counting her move to Loch Fuar. 'Open, now that you mention it. But my wallet's still in there.'

Callan grunted and held up a finger. 'Give me a second.'

He'd bandaged her knee, yet it still ached.

Callan muttered from behind the reception desk before returning with his hands wrapped in blue gloves. 'Hand it here.'

He studied her old backpack like a specimen under the microscope, running his fingers through its cotton fabric.

'Gran gave it to me as a present when I graduated. I love it so much.'

She fingered the strap that had come loose. 'Is it broken, do you think?'

She received a grunt.

With adept fingers, he searched the outside of the bag, as if someone might have hidden an important item in the fabric. Then he turned it sideways, and bottom-up too.

Was it an indecipherable manuscript?

'Don't turn it around! I've got my water bottle in there!'

'It won't unscrew the lid on its own.'

He assessed the bottom.

Small thistles bloomed on a white background. Aileen had tried so hard to keep it clean all these years.

Now, she huffed. Mud and some water from the puddles had splashed the side. It looked like she'd dragged it around a football pitch!

Done with his external analysis, Callan sat the bag on a seat. 'Mind if I look inside?'

Aileen blushed. 'You should never go through a woman's bag, Callan.'

'I don't care what it contains.'

He pulled the zip open and scrunched his eyebrows at the items. 'My desk would be a better place.'

The next five minutes were embarrassing. All of her personal items littered Callan's desk. True to his word, he didn't comment on any of it.

Callan pulled out a stack of tissues, Aileen's water bottle, her wallet, and a pouch.

Next, he pulled out Dachaigh's keys.

The keys clanked as he held them by a finger. 'I thought this set was always in yer right hand-side pocket?'

Smiling sweetly, Aileen patted her right-hand pocket and heard the satisfying clink-clink. 'They're in there. You've got the second set in your hands.'

And then it happened. The moment that made her blush like a beetroot. Callan pulled out a big, fluffy, soft toy. It had a keychain tied to the secret pocket inside her bag, so he couldn't get it all the way out. 'A dog? A fluffy light *pink* dog?'

Lifting her chin in the air, Aileen shot him a glare. 'There's no need to act surprised. I'm sure you've got a toy like this one.'

'Not a pink fluffy dog!'

'Leave me alone!'

Callan mimed zipping his lips. 'Our secret. Should I pinkie swear it?'

'Shut up!'

Grinning, Callan looked way younger than when he frowned. But the wide smile on his face promptly disappeared as he felt around her bag.

'What the—' He broke off as his hand emerged, holding a small pen drive.

Aileen squinted at the tiny thing. 'What's— I don't carry a pen drive with me. That's what the cloud is for.'

'Thought so.' Callan studied the black chip, holding it in the palm of his hand as if it were a ticking bomb. 'I bet yer assailant slid this in.'

Aileen stood and leaned on the desk to better see the drive. 'Guess we'll plug it in and see.'

CHAPTER FOURTEEN

Callan let Aileen work on the ancient computer in her cupboard-like room. The space closed in on him, but she'd said if the drive contained some corrupt files, better to sacrifice this computer than his.

He agreed, especially since he had no clue how a small pen drive could 'corrupt' a laptop. Blast, he sounded worse than his father!

Arms crossed over his chest, he stared at the computer screen as Aileen clicked.

She reached somewhere near her feet and plugged the pen drive in.

Five minutes of tapping his foot on the floor later, Callan swore if the drive didn't corrupt the computer, *he* would smash it to bits. 'How long does the bloody thing take!'

Aileen tutted. 'Come on, Callan. Patience, remember? It's a good virtue to have, so a famous detective once said.'

She was in a good mood.

Callan stared at the brunette. Thank God she sat there, safe and joking with him. He'd get this bastard for sure.

Placing a hand on the back of her chair, Callan leaned in. His breath hitched at her citrus perfume.

Callan cleared his throat and focused on the screen when a yellow folder popped up.

A few more minutes of clicking followed.

'Hmm.' Aileen grunted.

'What is it?'

She pointed at two files. 'One's an image and the other's a video file.'

Aileen double-clicked on the image and they waited as the computer processed the command.

The image loaded slower than a turtle's pace from top to bottom. Callan could make out a messy bed with clothes strewn across it. There were a few vests, shirts, trousers, jeans, and a pair of dress shirts and gloves.

When the entire image loaded, Callan squinted at it. 'This makes no sense. What is it?'

Aileen tilted her head. 'An unkempt bed?'

It sure looked like it. 'Why drop this thing in yer bag? It's got to have meaning.'

'Let's print this out. The image is too blurry on this device.'

Callan waved. 'On ye go, then. How do ye work with this piece of crap?'

Aileen rolled her eyes, tapping a few keys. The telltale hiss of a printer followed, and the device in the corner spat out a page.

Holding the crisp warm sheet, Callan studied the bed. What could this signify? Was it a clue or a hoax?

He rubbed at his eyes. They were growing heavy. He'd barely slept the past few nights.

Aileen too looked done in, but Callan had a suspicion she didn't want to head to Dachaigh alone. He didn't bring it up because he didn't want her driving back, either. Not after someone had purposefully accosted her.

'Should we watch the video next?'

He went back to his position behind Aileen's chair. 'Sure.'

The video took a while to load. When it did, it showed fifteen seconds of footage, just a pitch black image.

'Bloody hell! This is a hoax! Someone's taken us for fools.'

Aileen pointed a finger. 'Hold on! Let's listen with the sound on.'

Hitting the spacebar, she replayed the video.

A gruff voice filled the screen. 'I'll do it. Keep that wench quiet. Bloody women! They turn yer lives upside down.'

The voice grunted twice before speaking again. 'Aye, makes sense. Sure, give it to me.'

Another pause. 'Aye, I'll be there.'

A third pause. 'I'm not stupid!'

The footage stopped.

What the hell?

Aileen faced him, her eyes sparkling. 'Please tell me you recognise the voice?'

He didn't. The owner's voice sounded too muffled to make out.

'Can't. Did he sound like yer assailant?' It made little sense for someone to give evidence against them to the police. Still, there were some loonies out there.

'The man barely strung two words together. This one's talking on the phone with someone else. Hence the pauses.'

He'd gathered as much, yet a phrase in the conversation nagged at Callan's gut. 'Who do ye think these women he mentions are?'

'Dunno.'

Callan ran a hand through his hair, pacing the small room. What would he do to these women? 'Hell! I dinnae ken!'

Aileen stood and stretched. 'It could be Patricia or... Or can it be Fayola? Both of them?'

He thought it out for a moment, although the nagging in his gut persisted. When it struck him, his stomach dropped. 'What if this footage is new and someone's warning us?'

Aileen's eyes widened. 'You mean someone else might get hurt? Patricia? Or Hailey?'

Callan came to a stand beside Aileen. His fingers tingled, wanting to clasp her hands. He resisted. 'Or you.'

He feared seeing Aileen hurt.

What if today's assault had been a warning for worse things to come?

No, Callan steeled his resolve. She might be stubborn and strong, but he wouldn't let anyone hurt his *banlaoch*. He'd move heaven and hell to keep her safe.

❄

Aileen studied the picture Callan had pinned to the murder board.

The clock ticked quarter to one, and they hadn't spoken about leaving. She fought the yawns threatening to tear her mouth open. Callan wasn't so subtle about it.

He rubbed his eyes. But Aileen didn't want him to leave; nor did she want to leave.

To keep sleep at bay, she brewed herself a coffee and assessed the cluttered bed of their could-be killer again.

What did this person want them to find out from this

mess? Aileen couldn't see it, and she'd been staring at the picture for a while now.

The clock struck one. Aileen's eyes were blurry, yet she didn't give in.

The coffee disappeared in record time, and soon after, Callan's chair groaned where he'd been busy muttering curses at some paperwork.

He stood, stretching his arms to the ceiling. His black shirt slid up to reveal muscled abs.

Aileen's throat went dry. She swallowed.

Head out of the gutter, Aileen!

Her head didn't comply, though. A lack of sleep – she'd chalk it up to that.

She turned back to the photo and froze. Callan's warm breath tickled the loose strands of her hair, meaning he stood right behind her.

'I dinnae think the answer will come to ye if ye keep staring at it.'

Aileen swallowed, willing for her mind to focus. 'Why go through all this trouble to slip a pen drive in my bag?'

'He didn't want to be seen and got an opportunity when you walked into a quiet street. It's meant for us.'

She nodded. They had to figure out what it meant. 'It can't be a prank, surely. This person tailed me and dropped the pen drive in my bag, hurting himself and me in the process. What does he want us to see?' She muttered the last part to herself for the thousandth time that night.

All the items on the bed were clothes. Men's clothes: shirts, shorts, trousers and jackets. They were in a heap, making Aileen wonder who owned so many pairs? Surely they'd have to have taken their entire cupboard out.

'What's the significance between this and the video?'

He jostled to reach for the board, brushing his shoulders against Aileen's. The patch of skin where he'd touched hers ignited.

Goosebumps…

She wanted to snuggle into his cosy arms and snore. A large yawn slipped out. 'I'm sorry.'

Callan waved it away. 'Why don't we, uh, why don't we take a quick nap? If we return with fresh eyes, things might pop.'

Aileen eyed the uncomfortable visitor chair. She'd regret this later, yet she didn't want to leave. Besides, she was drunk with sleep, her eyesight hazy, her eyelids heavy. Her muscles sagged, drained. The adrenaline of earlier had worn off.

As Callan suggested, they sank into their respective chairs, Callan's searching gaze sweeping the room. When he didn't find what he was looking for, he walked out.

She heard scraping from the next room. Something screeched against the floor, yet Aileen didn't open her eyes. What did he want at this late hour?

A bang followed by a murmured 'crap!'. Aileen grinned a goofy smile.

His footsteps trudged back.

Suddenly, a chair thudded in front of her. Callan pointed to it. 'Ye can keep yer legs on it. Might help ye sleep.'

Aileen yawned again. 'Th-Thank You.' And the next moment, she snored away, feet comfortably suspended between the two chairs, and a smile at Callan's thoughtfulness blanketing her in warmth. She was as comfortable as she could get.

❄

Brrrng!

Aileen jerked, screaming. 'Ouch!'

A loud thud echoed, followed by: 'Bloody hell!' Callan had crashed to the ground.

She blinked the sleep away. It didn't take her long to figure out where she was. Nothing could be messier than Callan's office. The man in question cursed like a sailor.

She yelled over the screech of the alarm, 'Shut it off!'

'Sorry!' he roared back and promptly shut off the ringing.

Aileen gaped at him. 'It's bloody four in the morning – why's your alarm ringing?'

Callan rubbed his puffy face. 'It's my morning alarm.'

'It's not morning; it's the middle of the night.'

Their gazes caught, and they assessed each other's appearance. When Aileen should've blushed with embarrassment, she snorted. A moment of silence followed, and then they both burst out laughing.

Aileen guffawed until her belly hurt. 'Oh, Callan, you look like you've wrestled with a gorilla.'

'Haystacks look better than ye,' came the apt retort.

It hadn't been a wise thing to sleep on this chair, but waking up and roaring with laughter? She couldn't think of a better way to start her day.

They quietened after a while, their happy grins tattoos plastered on their faces.

Callan plodded to the coffee machine, its aroma waking Aileen's aching muscles. He stretched as he waited for the pot to fill.

Stiff as a statue, she followed his example, her sore muscles popping.

Finally, coffee in hand, they situated themselves in front of the murder board. Unfortunately, the clue behind the photograph still eluded them.

Callan gulped down his first cup, smacking his coffee-coated lips. 'What are we missing?'

Darkness still coloured the sky, thanks to the outlandish hour. Aileen didn't complain.

She set her mug aside and drummed her fingers on the desk. 'The video – the voice spoke about women?'

Callan caressed his chin. A prickly beard had grown overnight. 'Aye, women. We dinnae ken whether this is the past or his plans for the future.'

She held up a finger for each name. 'Hailey, Fayola, Patricia and Adelaide. Those are all the women we're dealing with, right?'

'And yerself. Our perp's hurt Patricia, Candace and Fayola so far. Hailey reported a break-in, but we know Fayola did that.'

'Right. So what does this bed or these clothes have to do with Fayola or Patricia?'

'There's nothing feminine – not a single item in this picture might belong to a woman,' Callan pointed out.

He went to the board and stubbed it with a finger. Standing so close to it, his broad frame blocked out most of the board.

'It's like one of those hidden-object puzzles. Ye ken them?'

Aileen grinned. Of course! She enjoyed solving them. Hence the sleuthing.

Muttering unintelligible words, Callan used his forefinger to go through every item he could see.

'White T-shirt, a red jacket with a number on it, a sweatshirt, a green tank top, black gloves, black T-shirt and trousers.... What's this?'

'What?' Aileen nudged him aside and peered at the image. A tiny black item lay under the jacket and another top. It glinted.

'A shiny purse?'

Callan tilted his head. 'Doesn't look like a purse.'

'It could be a clutch bag.' She drew a rectangle in the air and gestured holding it in her hand.

'It would be the only feminine item in this mess. Could it be Fayola's? Or a trophy her attacker took from Patricia's house?'

'It's fur.'

'Fur?'

Aileen pointed at the texture. 'It's shining under the light, and you can see the texture there.'

Beside her, Callan went still. 'Fur?'

Was he an animal activist? Aileen shook her head. 'It should be faux fur.'

'Or someone's *hair*.'

'Hair?' Her tone sounded sour.

'Aye, Aileen. It's a black wig – black like my hair.'

❄

AILEEN RUBBED HER TIRED EYES AND STRETCHED HER complaining muscles as she pushed through the door and stepped into Dachaigh's warmth.

Guilt tugged at her heart for not locking up like she usually did. All in all, Loch Fuar was a safe place for people who didn't go about looking for trouble.

Hanging her coat on the rack, Aileen grimaced. Why did her arm hurt? Served her right for sleeping in a chair.

She allowed herself a quick shower before tying her apron and getting the breakfast pans sizzling.

Inside the safety of her kitchen, she worked out the kinks in her neck. Her left arm throbbed where she'd fallen on it. Damn it! She had no time to wallow. Instead, she swallowed a painkiller.

Her exhaustion forgotten, Aileen lost herself in the job of fetching the eggs and preparing the batter. Today called for pancakes!

Grinning, she snapped an egg into the bowl.

Someone had gone to a lot of hassle to get the information across. Why the secrecy? Why not send the pen drive to the police or, better yet, come to the station?

The pots sizzled and soon the mouth-watering fragrances of pancakes, eggs and hash browns woke her guests from their slumbers, luring them to the kitchen.

Aileen had set the table and wished her guests good morning. They were all accounted for, except for Matthew Edgar, who hadn't returned.

She kept busy throughout breakfast, and the time flew by.

Aileen stretched again, groaning at her spasming muscles. They'd had quite the exercise this week.

Goodness, she hoped Callan didn't expect to keep up with their twice weekly self-defence lessons. When had they scheduled the next one?

Aileen shook her head. Not in the middle of a case, especially when they were so close to finding the killer.

There had to be a connection between the person who'd hurt Candace and whoever had murdered Blaine – assuming he had indeed been murdered.

Aileen bobbed her head and cleared the plates.

She wiped the table, set the cutlery in the sink and the rest in the dishwasher. Then, humming to herself, she rinsed the pans and enjoyed the stunning landscape through the picture window above the sink. The day bloomed pleasantly, the sun bright. Only a cloud or two hung in the sky, and the grass glowed a bright shade of green. Aileen was sorely tempted to ditch her duties and go lie in the grass to sunbathe.

Instead, she dipped her hand in the steady stream of lukewarm water; the droplets sparkling like crystals under the light.

This was the most relaxing part of her mornings, when she got to sing to herself and watch the splendid view.

Aileen congratulated herself on seeing the light and plucking up the courage to ditch her old boring life for this exciting one.

The pan clattered as she set it aside and picked up the next one.

Who had hurt her and where had they got the pictures from?

Someone's bed was a personal space. Who had access to such a place, or had this person sneaked in with a view to finding these clues?

Why turn those clues over to the police? And why do it via her?

There were so many questions, but they couldn't find answers before they found the man.

Done with the washing and drying, Aileen wiped the kitchen counters until they were squeaky clean.

Happy she'd completed her morning duties, Aileen headed to the reception desk to check which of her guests were leaving today and how many were checking in.

She worked out the rooms which were vacant and allotted them to guests checking in later in the day. Then she greeted the housekeeping staff, which was a posh way of referring to the sole teenager girl she employed. She was working to save for uni, and more economical than the cleaning company Aileen had previously employed.

Aileen was still clicking and scrolling through her emails when the door opened. A light breeze swept in, bringing with it an earthy smell.

Aileen turned to her new guest with a polite smile.

Her guest wore a long overcoat and a hat that shadowed most of his face.

What a strange person. His boots thumped against the stone floor and a low husky voice said, 'Ms Aileen Mackinnon.'

Aileen met his eyes, and her smile promptly vanished.

An angry bruise stained the man's jaw, a sinister shade of dark blue. His lips were split on the same side.

His broad frame was much larger than her petite one. And when he stepped nearer, she smelled the masculine aftershave on him, a musky one.

A shiver right from Antarctica sent her heart flying.

A step closer and a long shadow fell over her. Only a reception desk sat between them.

'I just want to talk.'

❄

CALLAN SAT ON HIS CHAIR, REFRESHED FROM HIS MORNING jog. The weather was perfect – not too windy or too sunny. Suffice to say, it had cleared his head.

A coffee in hand, he wondered what sounded good for breakfast.

Time was ticking by and before long, an officer from the PSD would be here.

Callan had to figure out whose clothes these were to get the officer off his back.

Looked like him.

Callan grabbed his notepad and perused his notes. Who'd said those exact words?

His calloused finger traced the words he'd scrawled. Aileen had said the man who'd been in Patricia's flat, arguing with her, had looked like him – or at least his silhouette had.

If Aileen and Isla had seen this same man there, then he had one connection between Patricia and what had happened to Candace.

What did this person want with these women? Did he want to destroy Callan's good name? Or was he bullying these women to keep their mouths shut?

He ran a hand through his hair as his stomach grumbled.

Bloody hell! He needed food.

Huffing, Callan shrugged into his jacket.

Some real coffee and a good sugary pastry would get him back in the groove, not that he wasn't upbeat.

Callan reached the door when a thought struck him like Archimedes having a Eureka moment.

Isla.

Her sharp eyes noticed what people wore.

He waited patiently in the queue, which always formed in the early hours, the printout of the photo clutched in his fist.

The woman in question bustled as her sugary treats and coffee greeted the entire town. She laughed and grinned at every customer, their usual orders ready before they placed them.

Thanks to the quick-moving queue, Callan got to the counter before his stomach conducted a revolt.

Isla scowled, her laughter long dissolved. 'What are you doing here? I thought Aileen was taking care of you.'

'I've never heard of business owners turning their loyal customers away. I was one of the first, remember?'

As Daniel's wife, Isla was his honorary sister. And true to her role, she bantered with him regularly.

She jabbed a thumb towards the door. 'Get your breakfast at Dachaigh.'

Yet she had a go-cup of bitter iced coffee on the counter and a strawberry-jam doughnut for him.

He clattered the exact change on the counter. 'I need a minute.'

Isla paused her flurry of activity. 'This about the case?'

She squealed at his nod. 'My office. Two minutes.'

He walked in and noticed the empty crib in the corner.

His burly friend must be busy cooing at his little daughter. He loved his wee girl to bits. Callan wondered what had happened to the boisterous lad who'd run riot all those years ago.

Callan plopped onto the chair, eyeing Isla's miniature food collection.

True to her word, she bustled in as he cracked the bag open. 'What?'

He drew Isla's attention to the image.

'What's this?'

'I want ye to tell me.'

'I might be socially active but I don't go through random people's closets and toss them like this.'

He guzzled the coffee, swirling an ice cube around his tongue. 'Ye get a lot of customers throughout the day. Some are regulars. Have ye seen anyone wearing this style lately?'

Isla squinted at the paper. 'I dunno.'

Callan refused to back down. 'Think, Isla. The man would be about my height and of a similar build. And they are a bit… modern.'

She tapped the paper. 'Where did you get this from?'

He sighed. Give and take, right?

Isla's eyes widened at his succinct rundown. 'Aileen! Where is she? I've got to meet her.'

She made to stand, but Callan hushed her. 'Aileen's fine. She's at Dachaigh. If ye can identify who these clothes belong to, we might find this man sooner. Or I'll have to go through town asking everyone.' He shuddered imagining it.

A hint of gossip and people in Loch Fuar gobbled it up and shared the rest. He wouldn't want to alert this man, lest he strike out in panic.

Isla bobbed her head and sat, face stoic.

She held the image to the light and murmured to herself as she went through each item.

Five minutes in, he'd lost all hope.

It was surely difficult to remember someone from the clothes they wore, especially when they were the latest trends. Almost everyone wore them!

He dumped the empty paper bag in the dustbin, wondering what he could do next. Everything seemed bleak.

Isla gasped softly. Her mouth had formed an O, and her forehead creased in a frown.

When she turned to him, her eyes glimmered with triumph. 'This wristband, I know this one. Where have I seen it? I thought how odd it looked.'

Wristband?

She sat the image on the counter and pointed at a small black band in the corner. It had a weird star on it made with some metallic material.

Tapping on it, Isla said, 'I saw this and wondered who wore a wristband these days, especially one so gaudy and clunky. One swing and a star that size could take someone's eye out!'

He gripped the chair, heart speeding with hope. 'Who wore it?'

Before she could answer, his phone interrupted them.

Aileen sounded out of breath.

'What? Aileen, what is it?' Callan barked when her voice cracked.

She whispered, 'Just come to Dachaigh. Please, come quick. It's important.'

❄

CALLAN FLOORED THE ACCELERATOR, NOT GIVING TWO hoots about the speed limit.

His heart clenched, shoulders bunched to his ears, and a sour taste sat on his tongue. What if his predictions were right and someone had hurt Aileen? Or she'd stumbled on a gut-churning scene.

Heart hammering, head throbbing, his throat went dry: a man lost in the desert.

Isla clenched the dashboard, ready to jump out of the car. 'I remember now! Cosimo Bocelli. This wristband belongs to him.'

Dachaigh emerged from behind dried tree branches, the white building a stark contrast to the green landscape.

He barely noticed the sweet birdsong or the fresh flowers on the windowsills. He didn't respond to Isla's comment.

They barrelled inside, feet thundering, and raced through the reception area into the living room.

'Callan?' Aileen's voice drifted through from the kitchen.

He followed it, heart desperate to beat out of his chest, stepped through the doorway and stumbled to a halt.

Aileen stood by the sink.

Isla bumped into him. 'Oh, thank God you're alright.'

Callan wasn't alright. The man beside Aileen wore a baggy overcoat and had bruises on his face.

'Jason Mitso.'

CHAPTER FIFTEEN

It didn't require a detective to figure out where Jason Mitso had got his wounds. Callan gritted his teeth and stalked towards where he stood on the other side of the counter.

The feartie hid behind Aileen, her petite frame barely concealing him. Aileen's soft palm collided against Callan's heaving chest. 'Callan, he wants to talk to you.'

'Is that so? Why did he attack ye then?'

He stood close enough to sandwich Aileen between them. And she didn't move. 'Please listen to him. I called you here because of what he's got to say.'

Callan shot a glare at Aileen. What was she playing at? This man had accosted her in the middle of a quiet street last night – hurt her. How could she ask Callan to keep calm and listen to his false words?

Her brown orbs were deep pools, pleading with him. She wetted her lips and tried again. 'He has some information for us. And he doesn't want anyone to trace it back to him.'

Fine!

Callan met Jason's wide gaze. 'Why? Don't ye want Cosimo to ken ye've been spying on him?'

Living under the same roof gave him access to Cosimo's wardrobe and an opportunity to listen in on his phone calls.

Jason huffed, dispensing a cloud of his strange musky cologne. 'I kent ye'd figure it out. I wanted to speak with Ms Mackinnon and ask her to talk to ye but… but I need to speak with ye and make sure ye get all the facts.'

Crossing his arms across his chest, Callan leaned back to study the man.

His overcoat drooped down from his shoulders, too large for him. Jason, like Callan, had broad shoulders. He'd styled his hair to peak in the centre, but now it stuck out, a wee bit askew, as if he'd run his hands through it. Heavy pouches under his eyes hinted at restless nights. He played with the hem of his coat and he looked everywhere but at Callan. Was he shy or afraid?

'Well, what arc ye waiting for?' Callan pulled out his notepad. 'Let's hear yer tale.'

Aileen gestured for Callan to take a seat at the counter, and she pointed to the other chair. 'Jason, why don't you sit there?'

Like an obedient puppy, the bulky man did so. Callan watched Aileen bustling in the kitchen, working out her nerves. A few strands of her hair tickled her neck. Her messy appearance warmed his heart.

Focus, Cameron.

Intertwining his hands, Callan leaned in. 'Whatever ye say will be confidential. Right, Aileen? Isla?'

Isla shook her head. 'Sorry, I've got to get back to the bakery.'

She waved at Aileen, mouthed something unintelligible, gesturing with her hands before heading off with Aileen's car keys.

Callan turned back to Jason. 'Go on, I haven't got all day.'

Jason looked Aileen in the eye. 'I'm sorry – I am. I didn't mean to hurt ye last night.'

'Why did ye?' Callan snapped.

The man had the audacity to shrug, as if it didn't matter. 'I needed to get this information to ye without anyone noticing me. I don't want to be the one to stab Cosimo in the back.'

A sweet aroma had Callan salivating. Hot chocolate bubbled on the stove.

He met Aileen's gaze, and she blushed. 'No more coffee for you. Why do you think Cosimo did it?'

The scraping of a spoon filled the tangible silence.

Jason ran a hand through his hair, dislodging it again. 'Where do I start?'

'At the beginning, and don't leave anything out.'

Aileen placed two mugs onto the counter and slid in beside Callan.

Jason ran a thumb over the rim of his mug, far away in his head. 'Cosimo's been acting weird lately. At first, I pegged it to divorce blues. It hit him hard – didn't see it coming. He came home with a bruise and it wasn't midnight yet. He hadn't been drinking, so it couldn't have been a pub brawl.

'When I asked him about it, he dismissed my worries. Then I saw more wounds on his arms. When I kept asking, he chalked it down to a job at Wallace Street.'

Jason halted to take a sip. Callan made a note of all he said, calculating the chronology of events. 'Do ye remember when he said this?'

'The same day Candace Willoughby got hurt.' Jason

rubbed his face. 'I panicked when I heard about it because… Because she lives on the same street and, well, as I said, Cosimo'd been acting strangely. So I asked him about it again – not specifically about Willoughby, yet he cut me off.'

Aileen stabbed a finger on the cold marble. 'Can you explain what you mean by Cosimo acting strangely?'

'He'd be on phone calls at all sorts of hours, always leaving the room to speak. We've been best buds for so long, we've never had secrets. Hell, I kent all about his orientation as a teenager!'

Callan halted Jason's ramblings. 'What do ye mean?'

Jason chewed on his lips, muttered a curse, and sighed. 'He came out to me about being gay, although he felt afraid to speak with his father. Why do ye think his father didn't hand the business over to him? They don't speak with each other.' Jason waved a hand. 'Recently, Cosimo's been too jumpy. We argued when I left the back door open for a couple of minutes. This is Loch Fuar, a safe community. He's become paranoid, asking me where I've been and who I've spoken to. It's not like him.'

Aileen and Callan shared a look.

Had Jason been lying? Callan had pegged Cosimo as a carefree man. What did he have to hide?

Callan's gut protested, and his training urged him to listen to it all. 'Do ye ken exactly when he became this way – his behaviour, I mean? Was it right after the divorce?'

Jason shook his head. 'That's what I find so strange. The day ye reopened Blaine's case – I remember because we'd planned to hit the pub after work. He didn't turn up. But Cosimo loves a night out.'

Callan tapped his pen on the counter. He sensed there was more to it than Jason was letting on. 'Go on.'

'He got a phone call yesterday evening, the one I taped.

Afterwards, he packed all his clothes. The picture I sent to ye? I took it when he packed those suitcases. He said he had to get away urgently.'

A bird wailed in the distance.

'Do ye ken where he went?'

Jason slouched, eyes downcast. 'I would have brought him back home if I knew.'

Callan flattened the image he'd printed out on the counter. He pointed at the wig, gloves and trousers: all black.

'Is this what he wore when he went to work at Wallace Street?'

Jason pursed his lips and thought. 'Aye. He dressed all in black. Another odd thing for Cosimo to do. He loves colour – hates black, too. And when I heard the rumours... He'd dressed to look like ye. He wanted to frame ye, Callan.'

❄

'WHAT DO YOU THINK?' AILEEN STARED AFTER THE POLICE cruiser.

Despite what he'd just told them, Callan had got Robert to drag Jason's arse to the police station. He'd accosted Aileen, injured her, too. What if she'd hurt her head or fallen in the way of an approaching car?

He subdued the fear before it could paralyse him. Instead, he perused his notes. 'It's odd that he'd tattle on his best friend. Though when I spoke with him before, he did mention Cosimo's odd behaviour.'

But Jason had access to Cosimo's wardrobe and could easily stage a phone call.

'I need to find Cosimo and question him.' Callan pushed off from the counter and texted Robert. 'The sooner I find him, the sooner I might figure out who hurt Candace.'

Aileen whistled. 'Would it mean the PSD investigating officer's services are no longer needed?'

The thought had crossed his mind and made his gut flutter with excitement. If Fayola's killer was the same person who'd hurt Candace and Patricia, it would mean he could close this case. He wanted to put it behind him, to keep the past where it belonged.

'I need to ken where Cosimo went.'

Aileen tugged at her shirt. 'What if Jason's lying? He went to extreme measures to plant the pen drive in my bag. Hell, I wanted to punch his face, but that blue bruise! Why hurt me if he planned to come here to speak with you?'

Callan chuckled. 'I don't want to haul yer arse to prison for assaulting him. Let's get to Cosimo first, see for ourselves.'

Her soft brown locks danced around her face when she turned her head sideways. 'He could plant evidence, Callan. And he could also dress like you. You're all around the same height. Cosimo, Jason and you. At least we can rule out Gerald.'

What did she mean? Gerald was a tall man. Not as tall as him, although in-built heels would elevate a man's height.

'His bushy eyebrows are hard to conceal, don't you think?' She trembled. 'Besides, isn't he Candace's doctor? She'd have recognised his squeaky voice.'

She should have been able to, though she was old and most people in the throes of terror wouldn't be able to remember exact details.

He strode towards the door. 'I'll keep ye posted.'

❄

Two hours later, he had nothing new to add. 'Cosimo's disappeared. He's not at his house or any public area in Loch Fuar. No one's seen him all morning.'

'Well, I looked him up. It's a dead end.' Aileen sounded defeated.

A frustrating dead end.

Callan drove a fist into his desk when his phone vibrated. What did Lieutenant General Warren want?

❄

According to the weather report, it would be a stormy night, but this afternoon, a couple of senior citizens hung out in their gardens or porches soaking up the sun's rays.

A few curled their lips at him; others waved.

When he strode down the stone pathway towards Warren's front door, he heard a distinct *meow*.

The stout cat had managed to climb over the fence.

Warren stood at the door, the feline in his arms. 'This thing still trespasses, Detective. I'm going to have to file a complaint.'

Not this again! Callan groaned internally.

It must have shown on his face as Warren nodded. 'My thoughts, exactly. Although I haven't called you here for this monster.' He gestured to the backyard. 'Follow me please, Detective.'

He'd been in Warren's backyard to fetch the cat from his vegetable patch multiple times. So when he rounded the house and saw the wooden fence, Callan grinned. The fence stood at six feet and blocked off the view from Mrs Douglas's house.

'The air smells fresh again.' Warren lifted his left cheek

in a content smirk. 'Not of teeth-rotting sweet tea and hardened biscuits!'

His voice carried over.

'Arse!' a female voice called out from the other side.

He didn't want a fight to break out across a fence. He gestured to the patch. 'It looks good, sir.'

'Aye. See this shed here?' The small rickety shed stood at the back of the yard, on the other side of the fence. 'He worked there all afternoon – I heard the droning myself, over the rain too.'

'Who was working, sir?'

Eyes hard, he pointed one firm finger at the fence. 'Cosimo Bocelli built the fence for me. I had back surgery decades ago, and the injury's been acting up lately. I couldn't build the fence myself. So he did it for me.'

The shed sat in the back against a shorter fence, looking out into the back alley. Cosimo could have slipped away unnoticed easily.

'How did ye ken I want to speak to Cosimo?'

Warren gestured to his house. 'I went grocery shopping and heard ye were asking around for him. He was here, the same day the estate agent died. He came in the morning and worked throughout the day. When it rained, he cut the wood in the shed.'

'Were ye with him?'

'No, I heard him.'

Cosimo's alibi was no good. He could've easily smuggled another lad in, paid him to do the work while he murdered Fayola.

He didn't have the strongest alibi, but Callan could work on it. 'Do ye ken where he might be?'

Warren shrugged. 'Sam Walker expected him today although he hasn't turned up.'

Callan thanked Warren for the information and

headed for his car. The sooner he found Cosimo, the sooner all the puzzle pieces would slide into place.

Where was that bastard?

❄

ON HIS WAY TO THE STATION, HAILEY CALLED. SO HE MADE his way to her place, surprised to find the store closed.

Red still blotched Hailey's face, but her eyes were less swollen. She wore a loose white shirt and sweatpants, her thin arms gesturing him inside.

'A colleague of mine came through. Ye might want to see this.'

She pulled up an image on her phone and showed it to him. He studied the receipt for polishing and engraving.

Hailey sat on the sofa and folded her arms. 'He told me this person paid cash so there's no way to know who paid for it.'

Callan handed the phone back to her. 'Did this person hand the chain over on the same date as the invoice?'

She squinted. 'I didn't ask. I told him to remember as much as he could about the customer who gave him the chain. He told me he'd hardly forget her.'

'Her?' Could it have been Patricia?

Hailey scrolled through her phone, searching for the correspondence. 'Ah, here it is. He describes her as a young woman, no more than twenty-five. She had blond hair, was lean and chatty. He says her long red nails caught his eye. They were pointy and spooked him.'

Red pointy nails?

He'd never seen those before – nor did he want to see such a monstrosity.

'Anything else which stood out for him? Any facial marks?'

Hailey shook her head. 'Nothing out of the ordinary. He just said she was young, blond and had red nails.'

This description didn't match anyone from their pool of suspects.

Like a pin pricking a balloon, the hope in his chest popped. Another dead end.

❄

DEJECTED, AND WITH A RAGING HEADACHE, CALLAN trudged into the police station.

Rory, his plaid shirt well ironed and tucked into his trousers, waited for him. 'What have ye got so far, Detective?'

Callan was in no mood to discuss the many dead ends he'd run up against. He was done in, knackered.

He couldn't refuse his boss, though.

Pouring himself a cup of coffee, Callan sought refuge in its bitterness before he led Rory to his office.

The board with all the evidence sat in there.

Rory went to the board, mind churning. 'Ye've got a lot of information also pertaining to Candace Willoughby's attack and Blaine's disappearance, I see.'

'It's all connected – has to be.' Callan ran his boss through it all. The syringe marks found on Fayola's body, what Edgar had told him, the chains, Cosimo's whereabouts and the pen drive Jason had slipped into Aileen's bag.

After what could've been eons, Callan sighed, letting the pressure that had built on his shoulders out. 'It's all a jumbled mess.'

Rory hummed, still studying the board. 'Did ye search Fayola's house?'

'Aye, we found her boots. They match the footprint

found at the art store after the break-in. We also found her old journals. They date back two years, last known ending eight months ago. The tech team said she'd switched to an online journal.'

'Did ye read it?'

He hadn't had a chance to, but there was a link between her death and Blaine's disappearance. What could he find in her journals except—

Electricity thundered through every cell in his body. Callan wanted to kick himself.

Fayola knew about Blaine – therein lay the issue. Candace and Patricia were the last two people, apart from Cosimo, who'd seen him before he disappeared.

The perpetrator wanted to silence these women because they knew an important titbit, a secret which would help Callan piece it all together – an underlying thread holding the truth together.

Fayola had figured it out, and thus the killer had eliminated her.

Adrenaline pumped in his veins as he reached for his phone. He needed those latest journals, and he needed Aileen to go through them. Who better for crunching data?

❄

Aileen couldn't ignore her instinct telling her all wasn't right with Jason Mitso. His flippant comments about Cosimo's orientation in particular had her guts in a dilemma. He'd slipped it into the conversation with caution, almost deliberately.

So she'd spent a good hour and a half digging dirt on him.

What did he do for a living? Data entry. What did he do in his free time? Sing at a local pub. What was his relationship status? Single, never married. And his criminal record? Clean. She'd gleaned this from his employer.

With icy shivering hands, Aileen had dialled the phone. Thanks to her former career as a forensic accountant, she had some connections. Aileen sucked at socialising, yet working in the corporate world, brushing shoulders with lots of people in one of the UK's most populated cities, she'd ended up with a few business cards whether she'd wanted them or not.

And now it had worked out in her favour. Jason's top boss and her former co-worker played golf together.

She'd seen others make connections this way, although she'd never given it a shot herself. And she'd never try again. She'd stuttered so much, but by some miracle, the man had understood what she was saying.

Just like when she'd kicked a murderer in his family jewels and pointed a loaded gun at his brains, her need to help Callan had surpassed her choking fear.

He was a good detective, committed to his work and respectful of his badge. She wouldn't let some scumbag drag his name through the mud.

She'd drag the scumbag in herself if given the chance.

'Bloody bastard!'

Aileen clamped her hand over her mouth. Had she cursed aloud?

Her phone signalled, as if judging her momentary slip-up. Smart-arse.

'Hello?'

'I want ye to look at Fayola's latest journals. Could ye get here in ten? I'll send Robert with the cruiser.'

Did she ever refuse good old research? And she could pick her car up from Isla as well.

With a new tote loaded with sharpened pencils, fresh

pens, an eraser, and her trusted yellow notepad, Aileen set off for the police station.

The building glowed brightly in the afternoon sun, and Aileen grinned. Loch Fuar was her home.

And this summer, she had played innkeeper to an almost full inn, solving crime and researching! She giggled with glee, anticipating the crisp paper under her fingers and the fresh ink tickling her nostrils.

She used to be this giddy before a new school year, surrounded by shiny new stationery.

Aileen tempered her enthusiasm by reminding herself that she was delving into a murder case. That someone had *died*.

The thought cut the grin off her face like a tree surgeon hackling off a branch.

Callan paced in his office. 'What took ye so long?'

She waved a hand. 'I needed stationery since you've buried yours somewhere in this dump.'

'Hey! Ye said ye thought the place looked cleaner the last time ye were here.'

Two days made a big difference. She hefted a new pile of paper from the visitor chair and dropped it with an *oof* on the table. A good glare shut Callan's gaping mouth.

Gingerly, he plucked a set of papers off the desk and handed them to her. 'I printed out the latest entries in her journal so we could mark out the important points.'

They could've done it on the computer, but Callan was allergic to technology, so she let it slide.

Aileen flicked through the dates. These entries went back a month. It made sense to cover as much as they could.

She read the latest entry first. If Fayola knew about Blaine and had met her killer, she'd have written about it.

Fayola had scribbled a few curses directed at her spouse

and written a bit about being worried about Hailey and Adelaide's impact on her.

She hadn't mentioned Blaine or her possible killer.

Aileen flipped back a day. Here she'd written about another argument with Adelaide, about her infidelity.

Her heart bled for Fayola. They'd been together for thirty-eight years, and Fayola still held some affection for Adelaide, although her anger reigned supreme.

She'd written about the commission she would receive from Edgar when she sold his house. But she hadn't mentioned the name of the party who'd enquired about it.

Aileen read and made notes until her eyes blurred. Hours later, her stomach growled, yet she'd gleaned nothing new from when she'd started.

Her stomach protested again and in answer she smelled the mouth-watering aroma of caramelised onions.

'Hungry?' Callan's voice boomed through the room as he dropped a greasy paper bag on the table. 'I got burgers and fries.'

Her traitorous tongue peeked out and wetted her lips. *Food* her entire being screamed.

Callan placed two colas, perspiration dripping from the chilled cans next to the paper bag. 'Dig in.'

And so she did. Her manners forgotten, Aileen wolfed the burger without a second thought to the mess she was creating.

She justified with a mouth full of burger, 'Missed lunch.'

'Clearly. Ye were so focused on these papers, ye'd be hungry later.'

He too was hungry, judging by the state of his burger.

They washed down their meal with the cola.

'What have ye got so far?'

Aileen dabbed a tissue over her mouth and disposed of

the soiled packaging. 'She doesn't mention anyone that could be her killer or Blaine at all. Do you think Edgar was fibbing?'

'If he lied, I'll haul his arse back in here. This is his son we're talking about. I dinnae understand how he can be so unaffected by all this.'

She *could* understand a parent being unbothered by their child's presence or absence. She swallowed that bitter thought and tapped her notepad.

'The day you reopened the missing person case, she made a list of suspects. Adelaide had gone out of town, so Fayola had the time to write a long entry. She's listed Patricia, Cosimo, Jason, you and her daughter's name.'

Callan frowned. 'Suspects for what?'

'She thought one of you might be withholding information about Blaine purposefully.'

'What I thought myself. Does she mention what she found out about Blaine's whereabouts?' Callan's eyes held hope, and Aileen hated to crush it. He deserved a break after all he'd been through.

'Sorry, there's nothing in there about him. Did she have another journal?' Fayola could've maintained a separate diary about her findings.

'There's one journal in her files. The rest are odd documents about the properties she'd sold and her bank accounts.'

Aileen wished they could discover a clue. 'Did you find Patricia's invoice?'

Callan sighed. 'Aye, Fayola had folded it in her old journals, but it's an invoice – there's nothing incriminating on it that we don't already know.'

He jumped from his chair. 'Hell! It's one dead end after another. Where is the exit to this bloody maze!'

Aileen could've asked him to keep his head cool, but it would've been futile. Her head wasn't calm, either.

Her phone chimed with a text.

The name flashing on the screen made her groan.

'Barbara makes a mean shepherd's pie.'

What interest did Gerald Erwin have in her? Was it because of her friendship with Callan?

Callan looked at her grimacing face. He frowned when her phone beeped again.

'Want to try it for dinner at 7?'

The instant Callan figured who'd sent the text, his jaw clenched and the blue in his eyes chilled.

Nostrils flaring, he sat back and turned his attention to the journal again. 'I wanted to run through this case with ye again. I guess ye're busy.'

'Don't be like that, Callan. He… Hold on!' Aileen jumped out of her seat and strode towards the board. 'Where was Gerald Erwin the day of Fayola's murder?'

Callan snorted. 'Why do ye care?'

'Come on, you eejit!'

'Dinnae ken. We haven't got around to him, what with all these missing people on hand.'

Aileen rolled her eyes at his flat tone. Was he jealous?

It gave her a thrill, yet her eyes went back to Gerald's message. 'You're right, Callan. I do have somewhere to be.'

She sauntered out the door, hurt, even miffed, when Callan didn't bid her goodbye.

CHAPTER SIXTEEN

The Senior Citizen Care Centre was a two-minute walk from the Kirk School. The stone building seemed old. Greenish-purple ivy enveloped it, and in the garden, yellow, red, pink, lavender, and orange blossoms glittered under the golden sunlight, their fragrance engulfing the area.

She knocked on the red door, which held a wooden plaque with the centre's name.

A youngish brunette with bright green eyes unbolted the door. She looked barely out of uni, and her enthusiasm rolled off her in waves.

She grinned at Aileen, her baby face framed with those soft, round curls. 'Come on in!'

Aileen smiled and ambled up to the counter, looking around. The combination of white walls and red furniture was cosy and welcoming.

'I shut the front door at about six. It's dinnertime for our guests.' She gestured to a glass door behind her, through which a group of white-haired old folks sat around a table, talking up a storm and roaring with laughter.

Testing out the lies she was about to spew, Aileen glanced around.

Behind the reception desk were small boxes holding crayons, pens, books, a first aid kit, keys, and letterboxes numbered from one to ten. The other three walls had pin-up boards overflowing with flyers.

The girl chuckled. 'Our seniors are an energetic lot. They have so many activities going on at one time I wonder how they find the time to sleep.'

There were a lot of activities: fitness training, Zumba, treks, craft workshops, dance workshops, culinary workshops, bake-offs and, cramped in the corner, a leaflet for doctor's appointments.

A jovial lot, these were…

Aileen swallowed. 'I'm here for – for my grandmother. She'll be visiting soon and I wanted to know she'll be well looked after regarding her health.'

'I'll help you. My name's Charmaine. What does your grandmother need?'

Nothing. She'd skin me if she knew I was here asking about doctors.

'Oh, just a regular check-up. She has bloating issues and sometimes complains about backache.'

Charmaine dropped her smile and listened to Aileen's bogus list with concerned eyes. She was fooling a decent young woman, but her hunger for answers overpowered her.

'Do you have a doctor on call?' Aileen blinked innocently.

Charmaine perked at the mention of the doctor. 'Of course we do! Dr Erwin's here three times a week. Has his own wee office in the back there so the guests can have some privacy when they see him. He…' The girl blushed. 'He's a nice man.'

Someone has a crush.

Aileen pressed her advantage. 'That's nice. When is he here?'

Ticking the days off her fingers, Charmaine said, 'Monday, Wednesday and Saturday. He never misses a day.'

We'll see, young lady.

'He was here this Wednesday?'

Charmaine clapped her hands. 'Why, he's here now! Should I give him a shout?'

Oops. 'Oh no! There's no need to disturb him. What are his clinic timings, did you say?'

'I should give him a shout. He'll be able to help you so much better. He has a way of putting people at ease.' Charmaine flicked her hair off her face, sending a whiff of flowery perfume Aileen's way. Her fancy nails glistened. 'He always comes after lunch and spends the entire day with all his patients. It's heartwarming to watch.'

Sure.

The door to the far left opened with a creak. 'Hey, Charmaine,' a squeaky voice called.

Charmaine's eyes lit like firecrackers on Bonfire Night when Aileen froze. Goosebumps pricked her arms with recognition.

'Hey, Doc! A woman's here to see you,' Charmaine called.

Panic rose in her throat. She didn't want Gerald to know about her enquiries. He might be onto her or worse, think she wanted to spend time with him.

Without another word, she swivelled and stalked to the door.

'Oh, but lady!' Charmaine called. 'He's the doctor. Where're you going? I didn't get your name!'

The door clicked shut, silencing Charmaine's high-pitched shouts.

Aileen took off at a run, disappearing around the bend at record speed.

Hopefully Gerald hadn't seen her.

Thank God Charmaine didn't know her.

Damn it, she'd got the information she'd come for, but it hadn't been satisfactory.

Aileen whipped out her phone and dialled Callan.

'Huh,' he grunted.

'Gerald's got an alibi. He was at the Senior Citizen Care Centre the day of Fayola's murder.'

❄

AN INVESTIGATING OFFICER FROM THE PSD WOULD ARRIVE soon.

The weight of Ben Nevis on his shoulders crushed him.

Guilt, shame, embarrassment: they all reared their heads, mocking him like they had back in the police college.

'One-legged Cameron is coming to catch me. Ooh, I'm so scared!' He heard the chorus as if they were shouting it right in front of him – as they had countless times.

His eyes pricked with the tears he hadn't let slip. He hadn't wanted to be called a crybaby.

After the first few rough weeks though, his tutor constable had taken him under her wing, and he'd saved countless lives or changed them for the better. Callan's chest swelled with pride every time he thought about it.

His team had worked the streets, even the brutal graveyard shift. He'd seen a lot and done his best to keep people safe. He'd never looked back or reconsidered his choice of profession.

And now it was all on the line because of one sick bastard.

His head dipped, chin tucked into his neck, shoulders bunched to his ears. Spasms of stress shot pain up his neck.

He had no clue where to look next.

A resident on Kirk Street had confirmed Cosimo had worked in her garden before heading to Warren's.

Everything had come to a dead end.

And Aileen? Off enjoying dinner with Gerald Erwin.

A soft, feather-light touch caressed his cheek. He dashed away the moisture.

Who was crying?

Hands landed on his shoulders and kneaded the tense muscles. 'You aren't alone, Callan.'

He moaned when the throbbing muscles relaxed and the hands continued to knead.

Slumping into his chair, Callan hovered over the edge of consciousness.

Of their own accord, his hands engulfed the smaller, sweeter ones on his shoulders. 'Aileen.' His voice sounded thick.

'Shush. It's alright.'

'I dinnae ken what to do next.'

'Rest.'

He couldn't, not when she was massaging his shoulders like a pro. 'Why aren't ye with Gerald?'

She stopped. 'Why would I be with him? I'm trying to make things better for you.'

Callan opened his eyes. Were her fingers magical?

His tiredness, stress and worries had vanished, replaced by energy; his thoughts clearer.

Callan swivelled in his seat to face her. 'Why are ye here?'

She huffed. 'I just… I want to help.'

Her eyes were so sincere and so worried. Callan stood to his entire height. 'I ken.'

'I don't know what to do.'

Did he? No, he too waited, stuck and frustrated, for doomsday.

Lowering himself to her height, he pressed his forehead to hers. 'What's going on in yer brain? I can see the wheels turning.'

She gripped his arms. 'What Jason said this morning about Cosimo being a part of the LGBTQ community is bugging me.'

He frowned. What was odd about being LGBTQ?

Aileen squeezed his arms. 'Callan, what if this date with Patricia was a cover? What if instead of Cosimo, Jason went on the date?'

'Instead of Cosimo? And Patricia agreed to it?'

Foreheads still pressed together, they were whispering to each other. Callan could see it now.

What if Cosimo hadn't been on the date? What if Jason had gone in his stead? And what if Cosimo hasn't accosted Candace and Patricia?

Callan straightened, missing Aileen's closeness instantly. If he sorted this out, he'd have a lot more time to spend with her.

Offering her his hand, Callan grinned. 'I think we should speak with Patricia. What do ye think, partner?'

❄

THE PURPLE AND PINK OF TWILIGHT WAS STREAKING THE summer sky as Callan pulled up at Dachaigh, right behind Aileen's car.

The homely warmth of Dachaigh had attracted its

guests to return for the night, like birds flying home to roost.

Most guests were in the drawing room playing board games. There were two guests in the library. Patricia was one of them.

Callan strode over to her. 'Ms Adair.'

Her eyes, when they cut to him were sharp, just like her tone. 'What?'

'I have a few questions—'

'I can't help you, Callan,' she cut him off, returning to the book in her hand. 'Bye.'

Anger licked his throat. He wanted to haul her in and question her formally. Damn procedures.

'Ms Adair, this will just take a minute.'

Moaning as if in pain, Patricia snapped her book shut. 'Sorry for this,' she told the other guest in the library. 'This detective spent his early days in a jungle.'

Callan didn't comment because it would lead to him shouting profanities at her. She'd baited him and was waiting for him to muck up.

'Well, can we have a female inspector present, so I'll be at ease? We all know what you did to poor Ms Willoughby after she accused you of hurting Blaine.'

The muscle in his jaw twitched, and his head almost exploded.

The soft hands wrapped around his arm centred him. Grateful to Aileen, he softened his fury.

'Please, Patricia. If you aren't at fault, speak with him.'

Patricia stared Aileen down. 'I'm under no obligation to speak with either of you. When you manhandle me, she won't stand on the side of truth in court. Why, I've all but lost trust in the police. Do you hear me?' she screamed. 'I don't trust you!'

'What was yer relationship with Mrs Noah?'

She ignored him, yet Callan wouldn't leave until he'd been victorious. 'Why did ye get your chain polished and re-engraved?'

Still no answer.

'Why—'

'Lawyer!' Patricia yelled, stomping her foot. 'If you have any more questions, call me to your office and I'll be there with my lawyer.'

Why was she being so secretive? The ruder she behaved, the more inclined Callan was to haul her in for this murder.

But instead, he left Patricia alone. He wouldn't talk to her without a lawyer. He'd give her no chance to slither out of a prison sentence if she'd killed Fayola.

He had better things to do, like hash this out with Aileen. Between the two of them, they'd come up with another lead.

They always did.

❄

Callan and Aileen agreed they needed his murder board to discuss this case, but not under the same roof as two of their suspects.

They'd zipped out of Dachaigh, each in their respective cars, and planted themselves in front of the board.

Aileen tilted her head, her throbbing arm forgotten in the excitement of working on the case. 'Why don't you run me through it?'

Their gazes turned to the one picture at the centre of it all. A frail boy of eighteen.

'We reopened Blaine's missing person case. It all started around then.' And they ran through it all: Candace Willoughby, the attack on Patricia, Fayola's murder, the parcel Ginny had received, the chains, and Jason's attack on Aileen.

'And we're still running into dead ends. Gerald has an alibi for the murder and Warren's championing Cosimo.'

He didn't know about Jason.

'Where was Jason that day?'

Callan waved his hand, sending a drift of his woody cologne to tease Aileen's nostrils. 'Practising with his band mates. They were drunk, in the middle of the bloody day. He could've slipped out.'

And he'd also had the opportunity to stage the picture and call it Cosimo's wardrobe. It was his word against an absent suspect's. What proof did they have it was the truth?

The man in question had gone missing, but they didn't know if he'd had run off or Jason had coerced him. Or worse…

Aileen swallowed the lump of trepidation in her throat. 'So Jason's got a loose alibi. And we were with Patricia at the time of the murder.'

'It rained heavily that day so ye could've missed someone dragging Fayola into the house.'

Aileen pursed her lips. They couldn't dismiss the possibility, yet it nagged at her.

Thoughts unfurled easily when she paced. Aileen had never been in the habit of pacing before, although now she did, her thoughts pounding at her brain for attention, boots clicking on the floor.

She halted mid-step and pointed at Patricia.

'The entrance to her house. That narrow iron staircase. Fayola was tall – she wouldn't have been easy to carry.'

Callan leaned a hip against his desk and scratched his prickly chin like he always did when he was thinking. 'As I recall, there's a staircase to her house from inside the store.'

'We were there, in the store! And you said Fayola died at around the same time.'

He waved his hand, stopping her short. 'No, there's a couple of hours unaccounted for. You got there at three. The ME says the time of death could've been two hours before. So technically, Patricia doesn't have an alibi either and she's reluctant to talk.'

Patricia was a spitfire, and not the nicest person Aileen had ever met. Daniel McIntyre had befriended her though, and Daniel's wife, Isla, could judge a person's character well, but then Patricia could be a talented actress.

'So she murdered her, came back downstairs and then took us up to clean her flat?'

Callan waved his hands. 'Ye'll be her alibis, right?'

What could be the motive? She was one of the last people to see Blaine before he disappeared. What did she know?

'Do we know anything new about Blaine's whereabouts?' she whispered, afraid to shatter Callan's peace of mind.

If the topic affected him, Callan didn't say. He moved on. 'Nothing we didn't already ken. No one apart from Candace reached out to us. And paying her a visit has come to bite me in the arse.'

She wouldn't let him blame himself. Aileen sat straighter, relaxing her tight muscles. 'Not true. We know so much. Someone amongst these people knows more than they're letting on and they're hiding a secret. In fact, they'll go to any lengths to hide it.'

'Do ye think he's dead?'

Callan had whispered the question, but it grew like a seed sown, until it lay there living and bloating in the room.

Speechless, Aileen reached out and squeezed his shoulder. 'I don't know, but whatever happened, it's our duty to find him.'

She swirled the helplessness into anger, a raging need to help Callan burning inside her. 'Hailey – what do you think about her?'

'A hapless wee thing lost in her mothers' battle,' Callan replied. 'She'd worked at the shop every single day. Customers have corroborated her alibi.'

'She could've slipped away.' Aileen didn't sound convinced herself.

'Aye, except she hasn't got a vehicle of her own to drive herself to and fro.'

Hell! And taking her mother's white van would be way too obvious. With her build and lack of muscle, she couldn't lift the deadweight of a body either.

Callan plucked Hailey's picture from the board. 'Not her.' He proceeded to mark Patricia, the pen squeaking against the board. Would she fake looking like a man to accost Candace?

Aileen mulled over what he'd said. 'No, this person had to have carried Candace – knocked her out cold before dumping her in your car. He did this in under five minutes. The more time he spent in the open, the more chance someone might see. At the same time, poison is more common among female killers.' Aileen pointed at Patricia's shot. 'Do we have two criminals?'

Callan caressed his chin when it dawned on him. 'No, it's one killer, a mastermind. Someone else is a pawn.' Eyes bright, he shuffled closer to the board. 'The killing's key because Fayola figured it out. Whatever the secret about Blaine, she figured that out. Patricia and Candace ken it too, although it's not the entire truth. So it wasn't crucial to… eliminate them as much as warn them to stay quiet. And having someone else on board also reduces the chances we catch our killer. During the times of the other crimes, he or she could ensure many people saw them.'

'Did Isla and I see Cosimo threatening Patricia, or did we see Jason… or Gerald?'

'To be honest, I don't peg Cosimo as the mastermind. He never planned anything. And Cosimo had a job in Kirk Street that day until the afternoon. He worked in the garden. The owner was in the home office, facing the opposite side of the house. A neighbour confirmed it.'

Aileen sighed. 'He had an opportunity to get away. Besides, you said he fixed someone's fence?'

Callan frowned. 'Aye, he volunteered for Warren, building the fence. I saw it.'

'And this homeowner in Kirk Street is old?'

He bobbed his head.

Aileen smirked. 'Would it mean Cosimo is a *handyman* for old folks?'

It struck Callan what Candace had said about the handyman hurting Blaine.

It wasn't Daniel Blaine'd had a fight with. He'd fought with Cosimo Bocelli.

Damn it!

CHAPTER SEVENTEEN

Aileen jostled in the seat of her car and let an uncharacteristic curse slip. 'Bloody hell.' Swear words were flying out of her these last couple of days.

Her eyes stung with unshed tears, her left arm throbbing something fierce.

Apparently, the effects of the pain medication and the day's excitement were wearing off.

Swallowing the pain, Aileen reached for her car keys. To her horror, her arm barely moved.

'Ouch!' She bit her lip to curb the agony. A doctor needed to check this. She had, after all, injured her left arm this summer.

Should she call Callan for help?

No, she was strong, confident, and independent. Besides, this case had frustrated him, yet with a dogged effort, he continued the investigation. Hadn't she just left him in peace so he could focus on it without distractions? She couldn't trouble him now. She'd get to the doctor and see what he could do.

Aileen eyed her watch. The hospital sat at the other end of town, and the day's activities had tired her out. She couldn't get there.

Driving with one hand was a mammoth task, especially since she had to use her left to change gears. The Highland roads were bumpy and jostled her arm repeatedly, causing her to shudder with pain.

After five minutes, sobs wrecked her. She should've just asked Callan for help.

Taking a moment to steady herself, Aileen signalled to the right and headed to Dr Gerald Erwin's clinic.

He's a suspect, Aileen.

So what? She'd been a suspect too, yet she hadn't murdered anyone. Besides, why would he hurt her? He was a doctor and had a reputation to uphold.

When she finally parked outside the clinic, Aileen dried her tears, cradling her arm as it pumped pain through her body.

Gingerly, she clicked the locks of her car.

Thankfully, it hadn't been her legs.

She trudged towards the clinic and abruptly came to a halt. 'Oh no!'

The medical sign flashed a white light on the damp pathway, yet the latch on the door didn't welcome patients. The clinic was closed.

Aileen buried her head into her right hand. She hadn't thought to check the time, and she didn't have the energy to drive to the hospital. She could barely contain the tears filling her eyes.

She should gulp another painkiller and have an early night. It was the logical thing to do, but lately logic seemed to have taken its leave of her.

A tear slipped down her face, her tongue tasting salt. What if the pain medication wore off in the morning and her arm jammed? Her guests would get no breakfast, and she would be stranded.

The sooner someone helped get the mobility back into her arm, the better. She'd read about this somewhere.

Aileen counted sheep in her head, wanting to distract herself, although it did little good.

With her good hand, she reached for her phone and dialled Gerald's number. How lucky she'd met him.

Fresh goosebumps erupted on her arms with every ring, but beggars couldn't be choosers.

He answered on the third ring. 'Hey! I was thinking—'

'Dr Erwin,' she cut in and explained it all to him.

'Why don't you come over? I live two doors down from the clinic.' His tone sounded soothing.

Thank God! Aileen looked at the heavens.

Her treads echoing on the pebbled footpath, she gasped and swiped at her forehead. Her hand came up damp. Another raindrop followed, this time on her shoulder.

Why did the rain pick this hour?

Huffing, she increased her pace, flinching when a fat drop landed on her hurting arm. Two doors could've been a mile away. Her shoulder pulsated because she held her arm at a strange angle.

Power on, Aileen!

A few strands fell loose from her ponytail. She didn't give a damn.

A few moments later, Aileen stood in front of a stone cottage. Thick ivy flanked the brown wooden door, the fragrance of some herb wafting with the wind.

Aileen shuffled her legs. What should she do? She had little choice, didn't she? She could hardly drive back with one arm.

She inhaled a lungful of strength.

Now the rain fell into a steady drizzle. If she stood out here much longer, she'd end up with a blocked nose as well!

Swallowing, Aileen strode to the door and knocked twice, squaring her shoulders.

You are an independent woman whose fought criminals and brought them to their knees. You don't—

The door swung open to reveal a man with bushy eyebrows. 'Aileen.'

❄

CALLAN CHECKED THE TIME. WHERE HAD AILEEN GOT TO? She'd promised to let him know when she got home, and she should've easily reached Dachaigh by now. Unless her arm had given her trouble.

He'd noticed it alright, and he'd had a mind to take her to the hospital. She'd injured the same arm again. Perhaps it had broken. She'd barely given it time to heal.

His *banlaoch* could handle it. She must've just forgotten to call him – or a guest had grabbed her as soon as she'd arrived.

Fifteen minutes. If she didn't call in fifteen minutes, he'd call her. He was taking no chances after what Jason had done. He hadn't cleared Jason, and with Cosimo missing, she could be in danger.

The easiest way to rattle Callan would be to hurt Aileen.

To think that Aileen was his weakness was pitiful – she'd lifted him from his despair, too. She was his weakness and his strength.

Callan caressed his chin as he perused the murder board again.

Anyone could forge an alibi, but there had to be some fragment which didn't fit, a mistake.

He studied Warren's message and recalled the layout of the man's property. It was entirely possible to get away from the neighbour's backyard, especially using that low fence between the two houses.

Had placing Fayola's body in Patricia's flat been a warning?

If Patricia told them the entire truth, things would be easier.

He moved his attention to what Aileen had learned from the Senior Citizen's Care Centre.

Gerald worked there three days a week from afternoon to evening.

Callan pulled out his map of Loch Fuar. He plotted Patricia's house on the map and traced it to the post office, the crisp paper sliding under his finger. 'No, Fayola would need to drive to get there and back,' he muttered to himself.

He traced the centre to the post office and paused. A five-minute walk. Callan licked his lips and gauged the distance again.

What was the distance between the Kirk School and the Senior Citizen Care Centre? Two minutes. And from the school to Gerald's clinic? A five-minute drive. And the clinic was on the road next to Patricia's flat.

Adrenaline pounded in his system; his vision tunnelled.

Gerald worked in the centre the entire day, but he had a separate room where he saw patients.

And according to what Aileen had said, this room sat on the ground floor and would have a window to slip out of, unseen.

Thinking quickly, he calculated the time. If he wanted

to kill Fayola and race back to the centre, it would take him forty minutes at the maximum.

No, no. If he timed it right, Gerald would've met Fayola near the centre. There were a lot of woods near the area.

He'd have killed her, then planted her at Patricia's flat to push the blame elsewhere.

Callan's phone rang. It was an unknown number. A sourness washed over him. He swallowed. 'Hello.'

An unwavering voice slicked down the line. 'Detective Inspector Callan Cameron?'

'Aye?'

'This is Charles Wyatt. Ms Mackinnon asked me to look at this symbol on the dagger. Now, it's very interesting, I must say.'

He didn't beat about the bush.

His blood pounding in his ears, Callan barely heard what the man said. He made sure they were on the same page. 'Ye mean the thistles and the sceptre are a familial symbol? The Erwins' insignia?'

'Aye, Detective. I think the dagger's owner is a man called Dr George Erwin. He commissioned a few pieces engraved with his insignia. He's a fellow collector, so we've crossed paths a few times. The door knocker on their house bears it too.'

Dr George Erwin's son Gerald, with his slick tongue and know-it-all smile, was a murderer.

The realisation battered his body like shards of ice.

Fayola had figured it out after studying the dagger. Did this mean Blaine was dead too?

Callan bid his thanks to Charles and dialled Aileen.

She didn't answer, drawing trepidation back into Callan's heart.

❄

AILEEN TRIED SMILING, BUT IT ENDED WITH HER GRIMACING. 'Sorry to disturb you.'

Gerald shook his head. 'No problem at all.' He ushered her in and, like a gentleman, helped her with her damp coat. He hung it on a detailed wooden coat hanger.

The entire house smelled of wood polish, something she associated with museums. Not very homely, was it?

Aileen stood in the foyer biting her lip, having second thoughts about her idea to come in here. The drawing room, as far as she could make out, sat on the other side of the doorway and was dimly lit. The singular vase in the centre of the foyer cast a long shadow.

What's with the lack of lighting?

A zinging pain shot through her arm. *Right, the arm's why I came here.*

Gesturing towards the doorway, Gerald said, 'Please come into the drawing room.'

Shooting him an unsure smile, Aileen ambled in. 'Um, I'm sorry to bother you, but I hurt myself yesterday.'

She glanced around the room as she entered. The couch and armchairs were made of rustic matching leather, antique vases and lamps decorated the small table beside the couch, and in the centre of the room sat a coffee table with an ornate antique bowl atop it. She could've been in a museum. A log fire crackled in the corner, its heat prickling her skin.

Her pain drowned her senses.

Gerald sat her down on the couch and crouched beside her. 'Tell me, where does it hurt?'

She pointed at where she'd injured her left arm a few months ago. The entire limb throbbed, tender and swollen. She didn't know exactly what hurt.

'I don't mean to sound vulgar, but could you take your shirt off so I can see the bruising better?' Gerald smiled kindly.

He'd been kind so far. Was he a wolf in sheep's clothing?

Of course not, Aileen. Being a doctor, he must've done this countless times.

Thank God for her vest.

Willing the trembling in her hands away, she unbuttoned her blouse and turned to show him the bruising.

Gerald reached under the coffee table and pulled out a torch. 'I keep this here in case I have a patient over. It's small and handy.'

Aileen smiled nervously.

Goosebumps scattered her arms when Gerald leaned in to examine her shoulder blade and triceps.

One flick of his torch had him hissing. 'You fell pretty hard, Aileen. And I'm afraid you've upset an unhealed injury too. Hold tight – this might hurt.'

A hiss escaped her when Gerald lightly poked her arm.

'Sorry, it's bound to hurt. How did you get here?'

'I drove.'

Sitting back on his haunches, the doctor pursed his lips. 'Give me a moment. I'll retrieve what I need.'

His footsteps echoed, fading as he disappeared down the hall.

The room was beginning to close in on her, so Aileen stretched her neck to the ceiling.

A frieze bordered it, a huge chandelier hanging from the centre – the sort she'd expect to see in a stately home. This 'cottage' was more like a mansion from the inside. It made her uncomfortable.

She slouched, sending her arm pulsating again. Hell!

The front door clicked, making Aileen gasp. Who was it?

Swallowing, she reached for her phone. If there was any hint of danger, she had to get in touch with someone, preferably Callan, even at the risk of annoying him with a false alarm.

Nipping at her cheeks, a heavy weight closed around Aileen's heart. Where was Gerald?

The lock on the front door twisted. Here, hidden in the shadows, she could see the foyer clearly.

Time stopped. Her heart raged on, thudding violently, her breaths shortening until she gasped for air.

Hands trembling, she waited, helpless, seated there in nothing but a vest. She didn't know whether she could put her blouse on again, and her phone had poor reception.

The door swung open with a creak and in stepped a hulk of a man.

Aileen's gasp echoed through the room, and the man turned to face her. The dim light caught his face, and Aileen whimpered. 'Oh no.'

Thinking quick, she fidgeted with her phone. She had to call Callan – Now!

The bags he held clattered to the ground. 'Don't ye dare!' he roared as he leaped on her.

Damn her clammy palms and trembling fingers. Somehow she managed to get to the phone app and click—

Aileen's phone sailed through the air and landed on the other side of the table. 'Why— Ouch!'

The bulk of a man tugged her left arm. Blinding pain ripped her apart. 'Ow!'

Don't be a wimp! Callan's reprimand teased her thoughts.

Swallowing as much pain as she could, Aileen tried to

punch Cosimo in the gut. It didn't work; her petite figure coupled with the pain didn't help.

Tears spilled over, her vision blurring, blinding her; she could taste blood on her tongue where she'd bitten it.

She kicked, but her feet met thin air, and a deep chuckle tickled her ears. 'Not so smart, eh?'

He pulled her ponytail, and all Aileen could do was flail her arms and cry out, 'Please don't…'

The pain escalated until her entire body pulsated, including her head. She saw another figure rush into the room. The doctor…

'What the hell are you doing?'

'Help – please…'

Bile erupted in her throat.

A syringe pricked her arm, and Aileen mumbled, 'Urgh. What…' Before she could get the words out, blackness enfolded her in its vicious arms.

CHAPTER EIGHTEEN

Callan knocked on Rory's office door. 'It's Erwin.'

His gut screamed a warning bell. *Aileen's in trouble.* Her fifteen minutes were up, and she still hadn't answered her phone.

Rory jumped out of his seat and whipped his arms into his coat. 'Let's bring the bastard in.'

Brrrng. The sound of Callan's phone made both officers halt in their tracks.

Seeing Aileen's name on the screen, relief shot through him. Where had she been all this time?

'Aileen?'

Someone mumbled, the voice hoarse. Fear scorched the relief. Who was it?

'Hey!' he roared. She should've been at Dachaigh ages ago. What was she playing at?

Callan called out to her again only to receive a grunt in response. Then someone spoke in muted tones, again in that hoarse voice.

Aileen didn't have a hoarse voice!

Thick droplets of rain slapped his face as Callan sprinted to his car.

'Talk to me!' Callan's voice boomed, yet he received no response. He heard a ping signalling someone had cut the call.

Blast!

The door to the police station snapped close as Callan slammed his car door. Damn it, he needed his SUV, not this flimsy piece of metal.

Rory slid into the passenger seat. 'Where is she?'

'Dunno.' His fingers grew cold and his limbs cramped. Callan's heart thudded a hundred miles an hour, beating out of his chest.

His boss punched him in the side. 'Don't lose control now! She's a civilian. Focus!'

Whirling his car to life, Callan pulled away sharply.

Rory let a curse slip. 'Can't we trace her phone?'

Callan huffed. For once, he wished he knew technology. A thought struck him.

Her arm hurt, but Dachaigh bustled with guests. Someone would hear the commotion there. Could she be at Gerald's clinic?

Dread enfolded him at the thought of Aileen in danger. He forced himself to move – he couldn't let his fear paralyse him.

'She must have gone to his clinic for her arm!' he roared, hauling the car round to head towards the clinic.

The tyres skidded against the wet road. Gritting his teeth, he floored the accelerator.

When he saw Aileen's fancy sedan parked outside the clinic, his feet faltered. She was here.

Callan brought his car to a shrieking halt behind hers and tumbled out, barely remembering to unbuckle himself, then raced towards the clinic. Gerald had locked the bloody place.

What the hell?

'Callan!' Rory held him back. 'Keep yer head on yer shoulders. Don't act out of fear. His house.'

The two police officers jogged to the stone cottage. Darkness had settled over it. 'Looks like everyone's out.'

'Hell they are! Erwin's a suspect and there's Aileen's car, right there!'

Striding to the front door, Callan pounded on it with a tight fist.

Rory cursed. 'Ever heard of being inconspicuous?'

Callan didn't give a flying fig.

Finally, a light switched on, illuminating the netted curtains.

A wild-haired Gerald poked his head out, his shirt askew. 'Aye?'

Callan wanted to pound him into powder, but Rory, being the level-headed of the two, placed a restraining hand on Callan's shoulder. 'Dr Erwin, we were looking for Ms Aileen Mackinnon.'

The bloody doctor had the audacity to look surprised. 'Ms Mackinnon? I'm sorry, I don't understand. What could she be doing here?'

Hand on the door, Callan pushed. The door opened a wee bit more to reveal all of Gerald.

'Her car is right there, Erwin,' Callan growled.

'It's a free parking space.'

Callan pushed the door some more. He didn't give two hoots about manners or facing dual complaints. He'd take on the bloody top dogs to save his *banlaoch*.

'Och, Detective. You can't force your way in.' Gerald chuckled and ran a hand through his hair. 'I might have to register another complaint against you.'

Callan had seen it – the coat hanger. And on it hung the unmistakable coat he'd admired countless times on Aileen.

Like a man possessed, he threw his weight at the door and sent Gerald flying.

Callan tripped, but righted himself as he barged in, yelling for Aileen.

'Hey!' Gerald shouted behind him.

Callan paid him no heed. 'Aileen!' His voice reverberated through the room.

As his eyes adjusted to the dim room, he made out the form lying on the sofa. Aileen… Yet she didn't respond to him.

His heart lurched. No! *No*!

'Oof!' The hulk slammed into him. Twisting, Callan heard the sneer and knew.

Cosimo Bocelli. Finally!

Scowling, Callan slugged the man in the stomach. The two men grappled. Callan was out for blood, possessed.

As an officer of the law, he hated criminals at the best of times, but someone had deliberately preyed on a wounded Aileen. He'd get his revenge.

Contracting his muscles, Callan growled, slamming his fist into Cosimo's face. The man couldn't match him – he'd gained most of his bulk by pumping weights at the gym. It all dissolved like sugar in water.

One crack across the man's cheeks sent him reeling and groaning.

Callan swiped the sweat off his forehead and flicked away the blood oozing from his cracked lip – it was the only injury Cosimo had managed.

Looking up, he met Rory's gaze. Gerald struggled, but Rory had him bound in handcuffs.

Callan cuffed Cosimo, then called the paramedics before finally dialling Robert.

Callan collapsed on the floor beside Aileen, his heart in his throat. For the first time he could remember, his hands trembled, not with adrenaline but with heart-shredding fear.

Why was she only wearing her vest? What had happened to her shirt? Had Gerald and Cosimo tried to…

He bit his tongue, drawing blood. It helped him centre his focus on Aileen.

He spotted her discarded shirt and fear squeezed his throat tighter. What had been going on in here? That bastard!

Was she okay? Blast, he hoped so.

His throat went dry as his fingers curled around her slender wrist, searching for a pulse.

A second passed, two… Nothing.

His limbs lost their strength, and pain like no other ripped through him.

Oh crap no! Not when he'd just figured—

'Aileen!' he roared desperately, refusing to think fate could be so cruel. He floundered for a pulse again. 'Come on, please.'

She didn't respond to him. Callan's arms grew heavy, his fingers ice cold.

Almost mad with hurt, he clenched her wrist.

No, he wouldn't lose her when he'd only just realised what she meant to him. Not when he was ready to admit…

Callan forced himself to stop trembling.

He tuned out the drumming blood in his ears, his frantic heart and thoughts.

Thud.

Thud.

He heaved a sigh. 'Oh, thank God!'

'Oh…' He buried his face in the crook of her neck, inhaling her citrus perfume.

She was alive! But her heart's pace had slowed.

When the room lit up with the red and blue lights of the ambulance, Callan shouted for help. He wrapped Aileen in his arms and carried her out of the door. 'Help – please!'

The next half hour whooshed by in a blur as Callan raced to the hospital. He clenched and unclenched his fists, but seeing the unconscious brunette had torn at his soul.

What the hell had she been thinking, walking into a suspect's house?

He didn't have the energy to be angry. His eyes prickled with tears; one slipped out.

He couldn't lose her, not now.

The moment the ambulance screeched to a halt, they rolled Aileen out and through a set of double doors, doctors and nurses trying to increase her pulse.

They pushed him backward, and the doors shut in his face. Callan crumpled to the floor.

Had he been too late?

❄

After a scalding cup of bitter coffee, Callan sat in front of a sweaty Cosimo, hands intertwined. He didn't speak a word.

Let the bastard sweat! Pig!

After a cup of water, Cosimo licked his lips. 'What do ye want to ken?'

Callan tilted his head. 'Why don't ye tell me? What were ye doing at Erwin's?'

Cosimo swallowed. 'He's a friend. He invited me over.'

Sitting back in his chair, Callan folded his arms and

watched the suspended light above the table. The clock struck every second with a resounding tick.

Cosimo twiddled his thumbs, patting a stucco on the floor with his shoe. Nervous much?

'Where were ye between 1 and 4 p.m. last Tuesday?'

Not looking Callan in the eye, Cosimo mumbled, 'Building Mr Warren's fence. Ye can ask him.'

No lies so far…

To throw the sod off track, Callan asked, 'Why did ye hurt Aileen Mackinnon?'

The bampot shook his head and stared at the table.

Callan knew when not to push. He didn't want this eejit to scream for his lawyer. It would waste precious time. He'd better change tactics instead.

Snapping open the folder on his desk, Callan pointed at the papers. 'So, Mr Bocelli, I've got a long list of offences on ye. And they're all backed by evidence.'

The bastard turned away and, like a petulant teenager, looked everywhere but at Callan.

Taking it as a cue, Callan listed them for him. 'Let's begin with yer latest offence, threatening Ms Patricia Adair. What was that about, eh? Trashing her place give ye a thrill, did it?'

Cosimo flashed his teeth. 'I didn't do it!'

Callan pushed. 'What about old Candace Willoughby?'

'Dunno who she is.'

Didn't he? Callan slapped the picture Jason Mitso had given them on the desk. A flicker of recognition flashed across Cosimo's face. 'Hey! Where did ye get this?'

'Why? Do ye recognise it?'

'Ye were in my bedroom! Who gave ye the right to barge in and take pictures?'

Callan ignored Cosimo's shouts and pointed at the black outfits. 'Hey, I'm just jogging yer memory. Ye are getting old after all, eh? This is the outfit ye wore when ye hurt Ms Willoughby.'

More sweat beaded on Cosimo's forehead.

He opened his mouth and licked his cracked lips. 'Okay, I did it. Gerry asked me to do it, for money. I did it, no questions asked.'

'How?'

'I was to dress as ye and attack Ms Willoughby. It would keep ye away.'

Callan raised an eyebrow. 'And?'

Cosimo sat quietly and then spoke in a muted tone. 'He gave me money. I-I have a drug problem and I owe people. He'd lent some to Patricia as well after her divorce. So when ye reopened the case, and she remembered she'd gone on that date with Gerry instead of me... She suspected him. Gerry asked me to go threaten her. Just a warning, he said.'

Bloody hell! What a mess.

He'd gleaned as much. 'And Fayola?'

Cosimo shook his head violently. 'That was all him! I swear. Look—' He tapped the photo of his bed. 'Go through the top wardrobe beside this bed. I have it all: emails, recorded phone calls and texts. I ain't an eejit. I keep records now so it's not my head in the wringer. Gerry murdered Fayola Noah.'

❄

Callan slapped the picture of the enamelled dagger on the table. He followed that with a picture of a syringe they'd found in Gerald's belongings and messages from Fayola about meeting him the same day he'd murdered her.

Then came the tapes Cosimo had recorded, and a

statement from Charmaine at the Senior Citizen Care Centre saying he'd sent her to get the chain polished.

Another resident had dropped in for a chat with Gerald but hadn't found the doctor.

Callan lifted one eyebrow. 'Need a lawyer?'

Spittle flew from Gerald's mouth. 'You don't scare me! Dimwits, the lot of you! I'm a doctor, I give people life like God. And like Him, I can take one if I want!'

Had he confessed?

'Why did ye kill Fayola?'

Gerald smacked the desk. 'Bugger off!'

Callan didn't bugger off. He just sat in front of Gerald, staring him straight in the eye.

Minutes passed, and a sheen of perspiration appeared on Gerald's forehead. Callan tapped the papers. 'I've got it all here. Not much can save ye from prison.'

Gerald curled his lip like he'd swallowed a lemon. 'I'll get out, I will. I did nothing wrong. That hag thought she could play me! Me! *Pay up or I'll go to the police*, she said. I sent her to hell! She deserved it.'

Callan leaned on his elbows. 'And what about the attacks on Candace Willoughby and Patricia Adair?'

Gerald flicked his wrists. 'They knew too much. A nudge and they zipped their mouths. But Fayola? She wouldn't. She had evidence too.'

'What did ye do to her?'

'Didn't your resources tell you, eejit!' Gerald jumped from his seat but couldn't move far. The cool metal around his wrists rattled. 'Met her by the school – it's a nice, secluded area. Told her I'd give her money. I pinched her instead with the same drug I gave your minion.'

'It didn't kill her instantly?'

'I wanted her tipsy when I drove her to Patricia's. I've got a key to her flat. Pat trusts easy. Cosimo had tousled her flat. All I had to do was ensure you found Fayola with the mess. A dose of cyanide and she died. I had the chain with me, of course – asked Charmaine from the Senior Citizen Care Centre to get it done for me. Blind lass she is.'

If it hadn't been for Aileen and Isla's sleuthing, they wouldn't have been able to interpret the evidence correctly. Patricia wouldn't have told them about Cosimo's assault.

Callan huffed out a breath, asking the question that had set these events rolling. 'What happened to Blaine?'

CHAPTER NINETEEN

Gerald's grin sent a trickle of ice down Callan's spine. Madness made his eyes glassy, and he licked his lips before he spat on the floor.

'Father loved that Asian heathen!' He mocked his father. 'Look at him, Gerald, he's scored an A! You must study harder like Blaine, Gerald.'

Fury, red hot, boiled inside Callan. Gerald hadn't been very conscientious in his studies, often staying out until all hours of the night. It all came back to him now.

He still ranted. 'That infidel sat on his high horse, smirking at me. Mocking ME!' he screamed. 'Then I go on a date with Patricia and there he is, preaching. *You're with Callan – don't do this to him.* Yap, yap, he went.'

Gerald slapped his hands on the desk. 'Enough! I'd had it.'

Callan's hand twitched. He wanted to reach out and smack the doctor until he begged for mercy, but remained still, remembering his friend. Blaine had never liked violence.

His boiling fury spilled out of his mouth instead. 'So ye

dropped Patricia at her house and went for a drive with Blaine.'

A lopsided grin bloomed on Gerald's face. He was a madman! 'You see it now, do you? Yes, we had a little chat.' He flicked his hands. 'Can't remember where. We agreed this wouldn't do.'

'Where is he, Erwin? Where is Blaine?'

The doctor sniggered. 'You're the detective. Find out.'

❄

SLIT-LIKE EYES PEERED AT HIM THROUGH HALF-MOON spectacles. 'Ye did good.'

Callan bobbed his head. 'Thank ye, ma'am.'

The wrinkled face hardened, and her red lips pursed in a thin line. 'I've taken back the complaint.'

For the first time in a long while, Callan's muscles unwound, free. 'I cannae be more grateful, ma'am.'

Candace Willoughby stared out on the pleasant day. The sky didn't hold a speck of moisture, although a tear traced her wrinkled cheek. 'I knew what he was going through. He told me how his group of friends were. And he also told me Gerald Erwin didn't like him speaking to the doctor about his career.'

Her arms shook more than they had last time he'd seen her. Beside her, her elder brother wrapped his hand around hers.

Dabbing her eyes, she continued. 'When he disappeared, he'd told me about his plans to go to the loch. He wanted to make Patricia see sense. He'd got into a fight about it with that boy… the Italian lad? But Patricia fancied Erwin. I'd seen them sneaking out of school.'

Callan didn't want to hear all this again. He'd barely slept the night.

Rage and arrogance.

Gerald didn't know where Blaine was. It just hadn't mattered to the bastard.

In the wee hours of the morning, Candace had called Rory, asking him to send Callan to her place. He hadn't had a chance to visit Aileen yet, and his skin itched to race towards the hospital.

'I asked George Erwin, the sick bastard's father, where Blaine was. And he told me.'

She leaned to place a sheet of paper on the coffee table. 'The address where Blaine is.'

❄

Callan stared at the sheet of paper Candace had given him. He sat comfortably in his car, but his heart was beating wildly.

He'd retrieved his own car back this morning. It had been a relief, as it had been to see Gerald and Cosimo behind bars.

With shaky hands, he read the address again. Did he have the guts to head there yet?

Not without Aileen…

He'd waited fifteen years. A day – hell, a week – more didn't matter.

He turned the key in the ignition, his foot pumping the accelerator.

He wanted to see his *banlaoch* first.

❄

Isla's green eyes held no enthusiasm. Dark, heavy circles underneath, coupled with a few silent tears she'd shed, gave her a haunted look.

Callan's hand trembled. Was Aileen not awake yet? Was she in a coma?

'Aileen?'

Isla blinked at his whisper, and a hard hand landed on his shoulder – Daniel's.

'She's in intensive care, but the doctor said she gained consciousness this morning, very briefly. She fluttered her lashes.'

His feet lost their strength, and he collapsed onto the chair. 'Oh, thank God!'

Daniel didn't let go of Callan's shoulder. 'She's still disoriented and sluggish. They're keeping her under observation today.'

His eyes shutting, Callan's muscles let go of the stress they'd been holding on to for a week.

'Her arm's back in the cast too.' Daniel gave Callan a side hug. 'Life's too short to be joking around, man. Don't let her go.'

❄

SHIMMERS OF FATIGUE CLAWED AT HIM. THE LAST TWO DAYS had been a lot of paperwork and calls from locals and from the PSD. He was no longer under investigation.

Another pot of relief.

Aileen was still in hospital, the doctors wanting to keep her under observation for a while longer.

Not being able to keep his worry at bay, he'd come to the office on his day off to work through the papers.

Callan fingered the sheet of paper Candace had given him. He still hadn't got around to it.

Not without Aileen…

Turning into his office, Callan stopped short. 'What are ye doing here?'

The cheeky brunette swivelled from her position in front of the empty board. 'I broke out of the hospital.'

Filling his mug to the brim with coffee, Callan assessed the woman. He needed caffeine around her or she'd drive him mad!

Her eyes were bright and her skin had a healthy glow, yet her left arm was still in a cast.

He perched on his desk, arm brushing Aileen's, and stared at the board. It gave him a sense of elation. He'd solved this case.

Aileen elbowed him, a small smile on her face. Gosh, she was beautiful. 'How are you?'

Callan chuckled. 'I should be asking you that.'

She regarded him and hitched an eyebrow.

Staring into his mug, Callan took a moment. 'Candace Willoughby knows where Blaine is. Would… Would ye…' His throat was suddenly dry.

'I'm your partner. Always by your side, Callan.'

He chuckled. Apparently she was. 'How did ye break out?'

Aileen blew a raspberry. 'Are you throwing me back in hospital prison? Because, Callan, the food's so bad!'

Now he was laughing so hard his eyes watered. He hadn't been this free since their self-defence dates.

Reaching over, he twirled a soft lock around his finger. 'Tell me, *banlaoch*.'

She patted her mended bag. 'I've got the discharge papers here. Isla was about to drive me home but I thought I'd come say hi.'

'Good.' His blues clashed with her browns; held.

'Never, I repeat, *never* do I want to see you lying unresponsive and pale again. I mean it.'

The eejit smirked. 'Why?'

What did she mean *why*? His entire bloody heart had leaped out of his throat for starters!

'Ye're a difficult woman, *banlaoch*.'

Aileen chuckled. 'I never promised to be otherwise.' She took a step closer until they were face to chest and peered up at him, her brown eyes lit with mischief. 'What's a *banlaoch*?'

'In this case, a devil.' Callan scowled. 'Banlaoch means a female warrior.'

His words gave her pause enough to shut her mouth. 'You think I'm a warrior?' She sounded breathless, like she couldn't believe him.

'Who else would get into more trouble?' Callan harrumphed. 'Why I'd…' He trailed off when she gripped his shirt and pulled him closer.

'Don't spoil my—'

The rest of his sentence dissolved into sweetness, and his mind went blank.

The softest pair of lips met his. He slid one hand around her waist and gripped the back of her head with the other.

It was the best sensation ever. Right there, his entire being centred, tethered to her, and they soared – together.

EPILOGUE

'Your destination is on the right.'

Callan's car rumbled to a halt.

Around them, a marshy peatland stretched with its pockets of water and grass.

It had been two weeks, and summer was past them. The air had grown colder and crisp, the trees losing their verdant freshness.

Aileen looked at her phone. 'This is it.' She pointed at the rocky fence between the road and the peatland beyond.

He'd finally had the courage to drive down to the address.

Looking around at the barren land, it made no sense. Was Candace mistaken?

Callan ran a hand through his hair and stared at it. Why were his hands shaking?

Aileen reached over. 'Hey, I'm here.'

He swallowed. No, he wasn't alone. There, in the middle of nowhere, under the blazing afternoon sun, nothing stirred.

What was Blaine doing here?

Despite having the address typed into their phones, Callan plucked out the frayed white paper.

Yes, they were in the right spot.

A sense of dread settled in him.

The left-hand-side door opened and shut. Aileen knocked on his side. 'Are you coming?'

He had to. He wouldn't chicken out now.

His legs were lead, so weak he struggled to stand straight.

A wrought-iron gate suspended between an opening in the low wall. It barely reached his waist.

With a cold hand, Callan pushed it open.

It was icy to the touch and swung with a groan that was too loud in the stillness.

'Careful, it's mushy.'

He held Aileen's hand for support, treading cautiously over the tall grass.

The virgin land was a vast area. What were they looking for?

Eyes sharp, he scanned the peatland – and then he saw it.

'There.'

Aileen squeezed his hand as they made their way over, boots sloshing in the sludge.

Callan dragged himself through the sludge.

Why had it rained in the morning?

He reached the stone, a tombstone in the middle of nowhere. It was bare, hidden beneath the tall grass.

Blaine was dead, gone, murdered.

An onslaught of emotions like needles prickling him from head to toe… Callan doubled over, tethered by Aileen's warm hand in his.

His eyes hurt and he bled tears.

Dry wilted flowers tickled the barren stone.

Fifteen years and he'd lain here all alone.

'Ye hold on to friends who'd walk to the ends of the earth for ye. When all is gone, it's they who remain.'

And Callan hadn't even known his best friend rested here, in an unmarked grave.

More anger for Gerald surged through him.

What jealously had possessed the man to have killed his friend in cold blood?

Aileen hugged him in her warm embrace, but nothing could ease the hurt. He was cold from within.

'You got him justice after fifteen years, Callan.'

'I just… I just wish I'd helped him sooner.' Blaine had trusted him. In a world where his father had turned his back on him, he'd trusted Callan. He should've asked more questions.

Gerald Erwin had cracked Blaine over the head with the hilt of his knife, watched him die, and buried him here.

The bare tombstone was a consolation Gerald's father had erected fifteen years ago. He'd known the truth all this time.

The wind blew hard, making the grass sway till it flattened against the ground. Clouds gathered in the sky, blocking the sunshine.

Would it rain now?

Aileen squeezed his hand. 'Don't, Callan. It's better late than never. You got his killer to justice. Even if he disappeared fifteen years ago, you never let him go. It threatened your career, and you still did your best by him.'

The clouds cleared, and a single ray of sunshine caught the grey stone.

'I want to give him a proper burial, Aileen. He'd have wanted it – deserves it too.'

She squeezed his hand again, her warmth permeating through the cold in his veins.

'The bird fell silent in the bog.' Callan pulled Aileen closer. 'He'd have done great things if he'd had a chance.'

She didn't respond. What could she say, anyway?

He welcomed the calm, letting the free-flowing breeze chill his nose and the grass tickle his legs.

There was a certain freedom here, but on a stormy night fifteen years ago, there was murder.

Callan watched Aileen's brown locks dance in the wind.

She was right. Better late than never.

Blaine could finally rest now.

The last two weeks had been a daze. Aileen's cast had come off, yet the doctor had advised her to treat her arm gently. So they'd hung out for dinner, movies, or chatting about anything under the sun. He'd laughed with her more in those two weeks than he'd laughed the whole of last year.

Callan swallowed and reached out. The stone was cold, with a thick layer of moss.

Shutting his eyes tight, Callan whispered a thanks to his long-gone best friend.

'Ye'll always be in my thoughts.'

After all these years, Blaine hadn't stayed silent – he'd left Callan a gift. In searching for his best friend, Callan had finally learned to open up.

He'd learned true friends stuck with you. It might take a while for it to soak in, but now, after being burned all those years ago, he was willing to try.

❄

PLEASE WRITE A REVIEW

Thank you so much for reading this novel. Please write an honest review for this book. Your review helps me as an independent author reach new readers. If you've never written a review before, don't worry. It doesn't need to be a long literary essay, just a sentence or two is perfect. And if you have the time, leave one on Goodreads and/or Bookbub as well.

THANK YOU:)

❄

Two seemingly unconnected murders, forty years apart. Would the next case get the better of Aileen & Callan?

Turn the page to read the next novel in Aileen and Callan's world

WHEN RED MIST RISES

Two murders, forty years apart. Are they connected?

Andrew Mackay is found sitting beside a corpse with a bloody stick in hand. Across town, the dig to unearth a body from the bog leads to the discovery of another missing person.

Amateur sleuth Aileen Mackinnon believes in Andrew's innocence. She's determined to catch the real killer, even as her own life self-destructs.

Searching for his best friend's body is turning out to be a mammoth task Detective Inspector Callan Cameron didn't expect, professionally or emotionally. Now investigating another murder and worrying about his girlfriend's safety, Callan is swamped.

When every move is like a step away from the truth, the only way forward is to collaborate. Who can they trust? Who is lying? And who kills when the red mist descends?

CHAPTER ONE

Finding your best friend was the hardest job ever. He knew Blaine lay six feet under, but where was the body?

Squish.

He doubled over as the mud sucked his boot.

Autumn in Scotland meant rains, the least ideal weather for treading through the peatlands.

On a freezing, rainy morning, all Detective Inspector Callan Cameron wanted was to stay warm, snuggled next to his girlfriend. But the job came before comfort.

His watch indicated the tenth hour, yet the sky didn't agree. Grey clouds hovered threateningly, blocking out all the sunlight.

Callan ducked to enter the tent and tuned into the crackle of the radio.

This vast peatland hadn't seen another soul for decades and now scrub-wearing officials littered the virgin land. Police constables from the other town, a forensic team of anthropologists, pathologists, and Callan as the DI all huddled under the tent. A few poor police constables stood guard outside, dripping from head to toe, teeth almost chattering, as they flanked the white and blue police tape.

'Dr Brown.'

The scrub wearing pathologist faced him, her face grim. He'd known her for years but never called her anything but 'doctor'. This was the new Callan, the one who let people in.

She crooked a finger. 'Detective, follow me.'

Callan huffed. Guess he was in for a shower, too. He bundled into the scrubs and set off behind the doctor.

Goosebumps-inducing drops of rain smacked against his numb face.

His heart contracted.

How can he be so desperate to find Blaine's body yet not want to find him soon?

Aileen Mackinnon, his *girlfriend*, had justified that finding Blaine would put a lid on the past. It would make Callan acknowledge the end of hope he'd held on to for fifteen years.

Dr Brown entered a barricaded area where brownish-red mud lay in a heap, along with bright yellow markers cautioning to tread steadily. The smell of fresh earth entrapped them.

Callan drew in his wet lip and sucked on it like an ice-candy. He took a moment, bracing himself for what lay in that ditch.

His best friend.

Dressed in all black, his soot coloured hair in a military cut, Callan fit in with the landscape. A lone figure amongst the red and blue flashing lights.

Callan squished his way beside the doctor and crouched.

She carefully folded the sheet covering the ditch. 'The

bloody rain's slowing us down. We need to remove him now. It would damage the body otherwise.'

Callan grunted, craning his neck to see the corpse.

Fifteen years it might've been, but the peat never let anything rot away. Blaine Macgregor would look the same, all these years later, like the Sleeping Beauty — unaged.

Fists clenched until his knuckles turned white, jaw clamped so hard he worried his teeth might fall off; Callan dared a peek.

A body lay, clothes covered in granules of mud. Bell-bottom jeans and a red sweatshirt contrasted the grey light. Curls of short strawberry blond hair tickled his forehead. And the face…

Cold shiver zinged through Callan. The rain, coupled with the breeze, had nothing to do with it.

This couldn't be.

'That's… That's *not* Blaine, Dr Brown.'

Her bottle green eyes sharp, Dr Brown swivelled towards Callan. Her eyes didn't hold shock, nor did the faint wrinkles on her face contort into a scowl. 'I thought as much. Those bell-bottom jeans I'd recognise anywhere. My mama wore those right after she gave birth to me. She never made me forget that story.' She rolled her eyes.

Callan ran a hand through his hair, displacing a few raindrops.

Oh crap! If this wasn't Blaine, they had a new body on their hands.

'Do we ken who it is?'

Dr Brown sighed. 'I called you as soon as we cleared out the peat. I got some preliminary pictures until you arrived, but I'll need time to examine him to give you any information.'

This man needed to be in the system for his fingerprint samples to work.

The temperature dropped a notch, making Callan want to draw his arms in.

Not Blaine. He still hadn't found Blaine.

Who was this man? Callan did a quick calculation.

'How old do ye think he is?'

'Judging by the fashion, he's from the sixties or seventies unless he liked older fashions.'

Callan raised his electric blue eyes with their hint of grey to the landscape around them. 'And no sign of Blaine Macgregor?'

Dr Brown pursed her lips. 'Sorry.'

'Maybe we need to get the metal detectors out again.'

Nodding, the doctor replaced the sheet over the ditch. 'I'll try to get the results to you as soon as I can.'

Callan dug his toes into the ground and stood up. 'Could ye email us a picture of the body? I'll cross check it with older missing person cases.'

A nod was all he got as the doctor got to work on removing the man from his burial place.

Callan walked out of the tent, scrub-free, and into the thrashing rain, letting it wash over him. He needed to contact his boss. After all, they had a new case on their hands.

AUTHOR'S NOTE

Dear Reader Friend,

The idea for this book had been cooking in my mind for a long time, almost ever since Callan told me his secret — his prosthetic leg. But as with all long awaited things, when I finally sat down to put pen to paper, I figured Callan's backstory was more complex than I had first imagined.

I started and stopped writing this story two times before it finally took shape. And despite the several words lost and dead-ends conquered, the novel wouldn't have been so engrossing and plausible if not for some guidance.

So as always, acknowledgements are due.

Thank you to P.D. Workman, Zack Duckworth, Harry Harris and Paul Gitsham for their help with police procedures and forensic science. And if there are any oversights, those mistakes are mine alone.

Thank you to my awesome critique partners, Janae Rogers and Kanika Bailey for your keen eye and insightful suggestions that made this story more impactful.

Leonise van Reenen and Jean Soderquist, my superb

beta readers, thank you so much for your valuable feedback!

And of course, the two people without whom the words wouldn't read as magically my editors, Laura Kincaid and Charlotte Kane. Thank you so much for your patience and sharp eyes.

This story was such fun to write. If you want to talk about it, email me at shana@shanafrost.com. I'd love to chat with you about Loch Fuar, Callan, Aileen, the other characters or anything Scottish.

Now, I'll be retreating into my writing den because Aileen's informed me she's in trouble again, having discovered another murder. She says she needs my help in solving it. What a handful! (Cue eye roll)

Got to go now, but I'll see you soon with another Aileen and Callan adventure!

Until next time

Happy Reading!

Shana

ABOUT THE AUTHOR

Are you looking to solve murders? Perfect, Shana loves plotting them.

As a debut writer, Shana Frost is in her secret den hatching murders and having a blast with Aileen and the gang. It's crazy in there...

When not in the den, Shana always has her nose buried between the pages of a fiction novel. After all, the tantalising aroma of a story is far more enticing, especially for a sensitive nose like hers.

Shana's powerful sense of smell has helped her sniff out murder mysteries and a wide variety of characters.

Occasionally, she finds herself wandering ancient hallways of a castle, or a museum trying to smell the tales these walls effuse.

The traveller Ibn Battuta wasn't wrong when he wrote, "Travelling - It leaves you speechless, then turns you into a storyteller"

Visit the website for more: https://shanafrost.com

9 789354 932533

Printed at Repro India Ltd.